Conscious Calm

Keys to Freedom from Stress and Worry

Laura Maciuika Ed.D.

TAP INTO
FREEDOM
PUBLISHING

Tap Into Freedom Publishing
Oakland, CA

Conscious Calm:
Keys to Freedom from Stress and Worry
by Laura Maciuika, Ed.D.
Tap Into Freedom Publishing
4096 Piedmont Ave., Suite 365
Oakland, CA 94611
Orders@TapIntoFreedomPublishing.com; www.TIFPub.com

Disclaimer
The information in this book is not to be used to treat or diagnose any particular physical or emotional condition. This work is sold with the understanding that neither the Author nor the Publisher is engaged in providing professional advice or services to an individual reader. The ideas, techniques, and suggestions provided in this book are provided for informational purposes only, and are not intended as a substitute for consultation with a professional health care provider. Neither the Author nor the Publisher shall be liable from any loss or damages arising from any information or suggestion within this book. The mention of organizations or websites in this work as citations and/or sources of further information does not imply endorsement by the Author or Publisher of any information or recommendations that may be found on such websites or in those works. While every attempt has been made to provide accurate internet addresses in this work at the time of publication, some websites may change addresses or no longer exist at the time the work is read.

Cover design by George Foster.

ISBN 978-1-937749-02-6
Library of Congress Control Number: 2011939452

Library of Congress Subject Headings:
Self-actualization – Psychology
Stress (Psychology)
Stress Management
Mind and body therapies
Energy psychology
Success – Psychological aspects
Mindfulness-based cognitive therapy
Includes bibliographical references and index

Advance Praise

"*Conscious Calm* distills an amazing breadth of information into a readable, practical mini-manual. This is the must-read book if you want to bust stress and experience lasting calm and peace in your life."

> ~ **Marci Shimoff**, *NY Times* bestselling author of *Happy for No Reason* and *Love for No Reason*

"Combining the neuroscience of stress and emotions with leading edge energy psychology, Laura Maciuika presents simple step-by-step ways to reframe our minds to choose calmness. *Conscious Calm* is a gift to adrenaline junkies who create their own crises and anyone looking to reclaim their natural bliss---a wonderful book that can change your life."

> ~ **Candace Pert, Ph.D.**, Chief Scientific Officer, RAPID Laboratories; author of *Molecules of Emotion* and *Everything You Need to Know to Feel Go(o)d*

"Integrating Eastern wisdom with Western science, this book gives you step by step, clearly explained procedures to rid yourself of stress. Dr. Maciuika is brilliant in the way she created simple, brief routines to enrich and enhance everyone's life. This book is a must read for everyone and essential to those in the helping professions such as therapists, physicians, nurses, teachers and coaches."

> ~ **Cloé Madanes**, author of *Relationship Breakthrough* and *Strategic Family Therapy*; President of the Robbins-Madanes Center and Robbins-Madanes Training

"This book by Laura Maciuika, Ed.D., *Conscious Calm: Keys to Freedom From Stress and Worry* is an excellent book for every human to read and seriously practice because our modern world puts everyone into an information, work and stressor overload. Via an easily understood literary style, she lays out a major present day human pathology and provides a straightforward inner-self management solution that everyone can beneficially follow."

- **William A. Tiller, Ph.D.**, Professor Emeritus,
  Stanford University Department of Materials Science
  and Engineering; author of *Science and Human
  Transformation*.

"In plain language, Conscious Calm demystifies inner stress and gives us a simple, clear roadmap to transform stress, reclaim our energy and power, and experience more calm. While this book could be a textbook to learning about how stress works, it is so practical, its greatest gift is as a guide to real actions anyone can take. We should all keep a copy close at hand. I will."

- **Rev. angel Kyodo williams**, author of *Being Black:
  Zen and the Art of Living with Fearlessness and Grace*;
  Founder of the Center for Transformative Change,
  http://transformativechange.org and
  http://angelkyodowilliams.com

"Did you ever have a friend who could always calm you down, and make you remember that you can handle and even enjoy your life? *Conscious Calm* reminds me of that friend, and what's better, this book has suggestions that help you be that friend to yourself. Dr. Maciuika's words are clear and sound, without the clichés you've heard that sound good but don't seem to stick in real life. *Conscious Calm* reminds us that – like the key we think we lost and, after a panicked search, find in our very hand – feeling good is always available to us if we know where and how to look."

- **Dr. George Russell, D.C.**, Bodyworker, Lecturer and
  teacher at the Atlantic Theater Company (New York
  University), Swedish Massage Institute and Kripalu
  Center for Yoga and Health. www.georgerusselldc.com

"*Conscious Calm* is like the handbook to the brain, body and emotions no one gets when they 'grow up'. I wish I had this book when I turned 13. I am sure that I will continue to go back to it for years to come."

> ~ **Sheela Bringi**, musician. www.shebrings.com

"In *Conscious Calm* you will learn powerful and practical skills to help you manage stress. Dr. Laura Maciuika takes you on the inside journey of transformation from stressed to calm. I highly recommend this book to anyone who wants or needs to bring more serenity into his or her life."

> ~ Ruth Gerath, author of *From Hired to Happy: The Secrets to a Vibrant Career and Fulfilling Life.*
> www.gerath.com

"Dr. Laura Maciuika has written a fresh, original book about our current stress epidemic. Following a cogent analysis of the dynamics of stress, she presents innovative strategies for interrupting the stress cycle, letting go of our stories and the emotional dramas they create, to experience the Beingness that is always already there. Resilience and flexibility, like stress, are inside jobs; *Conscious Calm* is an eminently practical and intelligent roadmap for living a happier, healthier, more stress-free life."

> ~ **John Freedom**, CEHP, www.johnfreedom.com

"*Conscious Calm* is a practical, engaging book for people who are interested in learning simple, effective methods to regulate stress of all kinds. Dr. Maciuika presents a complete, helpful program that is geared for success. With the complimentary "Try This" Action Steps, Conscious Calm offers a dynamic learning package that maximizes opportunities for permanent change."

> ~ **Maggie Phillips, Ph.D.**, author of *Reversing Chronic Pain, Finding the Energy to Heal,* and (with Peter Levine) *Freedom from Pain* (2010, Sounds True).

"What an awesome, straightforward and practical book. I'll be recommending it to all my friends and colleagues!"

> ~ **Mariann Mohos**, author of *You Want WHAT??? Concierge Tales from the Men and Women who Make Las Vegas Dreams Come True.*
> www.lasvegasconciergestories.com

Contents

Introduction

What This Book Is and Is Not About

Writing about stress is not a simple matter. Although high stress is often treated as if it's a personal problem that individuals should just learn to deal with better, chronic high stress is both layered and complex.

There is the internal experience of stress that is complicated on its own. While some stress is healthy and needed to be able to act in the world, or to change and grow, chronic or negative high stress can be overwhelming, and can include serious physical and emotional symptoms.

Outside dynamics and events in many people's lives also create ongoing, daunting stress. A discussion of complex current and historical issues—including global and individual financial crises, social systems or family dynamics that pressure those considered somehow "other," and the stress of working too many jobs or not having a job at all—would take volumes of books. But it is important to note here that many forms of ongoing, external stress can also lead to physical and emotional stress symptoms and negative health effects.[1, 2, 3, 4]

In *Conscious Calm*, I do not pretend to take on or overlook all the real outside pressures that create negative stress for so many. Instead, this book looks at where we as individuals *do* have control and choice, moment to moment. We will use a working definition of negative stress that includes the meaning we make of the stressful external and internal events and states we experience. This will allow us to explore what occurs within that affects how we experience both stress and calm. We will be highlighting the realities and possibilities of choices.

Even with outside pressures and realities, as human beings we do have choice and power in the meaning we make of our experiences, and how we treat ourselves in our internal self-talk and choices. In *Conscious Calm* we will address these inner dynamics. We'll break down the inside patterns that can make stressful experiences even worse, affecting everything from our health, to our relationships, to our level of happiness and success. We will explore ways to weaken old internal stress habits, and how to open the door to a new level of calm, internal control, and personal power.

How to Get the Most Out of This Book

As someone who teaches people how to experience greater freedom, happiness and success in their lives, I come to our conversation here with a particular bias. I want you to experience real and lasting relief from stress and worry, and to be able to have greater Conscious Calm in your life. I don't want this to be another book you read or skim, then say to yourself, "Yeah, that's interesting," and move on without anything much changing in your life. I want this to be the beginning of a real shift for you. I'd like you to experience greater ease through using the information in this book, and to find new directions toward greater inner peace and personal power in your life.

With that in mind, I'm going to suggest a few things to help you get the most out of this book.

1. Go through the chapters in order. Even if you think you know some of the information, this book is designed in a certain order so you can quickly and easily get the most benefit.

2. Be ready for some of your ways of thinking about things to be challenged—see if you can just go with it! Your ideas and ways of seeing the world may be stretched a little or a lot—that's how we grow as human beings and bring our life to the next level. We can't keep thinking the same stuff and doing the same things and expect our life to miraculously give us something new and different. As you read, be aware that you'll sometimes notice:

   • **Paradox** – when something that seems impossible or untrue actually becomes possible and makes perfect sense once you have new information.

   • **Figure-ground shifts** – when what used to be the background is suddenly brought forward and grabs your attention. At the same time, what seemed most important suddenly ends up in the background and less significant.

   • **World view blends** – we all walk around with certain world views or beliefs about how things are. We usually don't even notice them. These world views can be perspectives based on certain knowledge. In many cases other perspectives and realities exist as well. In *Conscious Calm* we will blend some Western perspectives and knowledge of the human body and emotions with Eastern perspectives and knowledge. We'll end up with a more complete picture that can help you be more effective in eliminating toxic stress and worry.

3. At the end of each chapter, you will find a "Try This" section. Each suggestion comes from the information in that chapter, and is designed to build your stress-busting muscles and your foundation for Conscious Calm.

I know it's natural to read the "Try This" and keep going, but to get the most out of this book, don't do that! Stop and do the exercise.

To support you in following through, I created a *Try This Action Steps* document for you. This gives you all of the Try This exercises in one place, plus additional questions, tips and hints for each chapter. You can then keep this on a computer, or print out the sheets for yourself and write your responses and thoughts there. Download your complimentary copy now at:

http://consciouscalm.com/trythis

Just reading about something is never as powerful as taking action and having your own experience with it. So when you get to the end of each chapter, do yourself a favor – take action and do the "Try This." You will reduce your stress faster and be well on your way to Conscious Calm.

4. Try to keep an open mind. There may be some ideas and techniques presented here that are familiar to you, and others that seem unfamiliar or weird. Again, we can't solve our problems or stress doing the same old things in the same old ways. There may be some new information and approaches here. Try them on; stretch your comfort zone a little if you need to. You will reap the benefit of taking in new knowledge that can help you free yourself from stress and worry.

1

Stress and Worry

Outside and Inside Stress

"I'm so stressed out!!"

This common complaint is often followed by examples of tasks, deadlines, challenges with friends or family, money, or job problems that are causing high stress and lots of worry.

Sound familiar? Most people will understand exactly what you mean if you say you're stressed or are feeling stressed out. That's true even though there is little agreement about what "stress" is among those studying stress and writing about it.[5]

So how does that negative kind of stress build up into feeling stressed out? And what connects outside stress with feeling stressed on the inside?

For many stressed people, the line seems direct. The greater the outside stress, the more I feel stressed out, and that's it. The more I feel pressures from the outside, and the more tasks that pile up, the more I feel stretched thin, tired, and out of control. Then I may worry at night and get less sleep, which makes me even more tired and stressed. And around and around the stress cycle goes.

You may know your own version of this cycle. This stress cycle is a common pattern for many people who are trying hard and are under real strains from the outside. Bills may be piling up, someone may have health issues, or big decisions may have to be made. Pressures from family or greater society, or stress from big changes, wanted or unwanted, can add up. Even positive, desired life changes can be stressful and leave people feeling stressed out.

Obviously, some external stresses and pressures are not under our direct control. For stress reduction, it's natural to focus on where and how we do have control over outside stress. Some people try to organize themselves better, or to break the To-Do list down into smaller pieces to get more done. You probably have heard about or even tried tips and strategies for organizing the tasks and To-Dos in your life, and doing that can be helpful.

Those tips and strategies take one common approach to focusing on stress reduction. They look at the outside challenges and strategize ways to deal with them better. And that can be a useful and worthy exercise.

It can become a problem, though, if outside solutions to stress are the only focus. It can feel like you'll have to get a handle on *everything* in your life before your stress will go down and you will feel calmer and happier. Or, it can seem like you'll *never* get less stressed and worried, because the To-Do list and the serious outside challenges just aren't going away anytime soon.

One reason some people feel both helpless and hopeless about stress is that their focus is only on the outside. Without addressing inside stress directly, without a better understanding of its dynamics, causes, and possible solutions, it's hard to find real and lasting calm. Without learning more about the internal contributions to stress, it's more likely you will stay stuck in some of the very patterns that can be making your stress worse.

While there are real ways to control some of our outside stress, INSIDE is where we can have the *most* control. Even with the real outside challenges and pressures, moment-to-moment we have all kinds of internal choice.

Although inside is where we have the greatest chance for choice and personal power, many people have little knowledge about these internal dynamics. A recent survey across the United States found that many people believed their biggest problems in dealing with stress were being too tired, and a lack of willpower. They named their outside challenges with stress, like over-eating or not getting enough sleep. They also knew what they "should" change on the outside to decrease their stress and feel better. But a majority in the survey believed they were too busy or low-energy to make those outside changes, and many believed they did not have the willpower to do so.[6]

Reducing stress by making outside changes can feel daunting and even impossible to someone who is already stressed out and weary. It can feel like putting additional things on a To-Do list that is already scary and too long.

Here, we will take a different approach to reducing stress. We will explore where you DO have internal choice and control, and where and how to make the choices that can calm your body and mind in ways that last. You will discover how the path to calm can also be the path to greater personal power and happiness.

How Did We Get So Good at This?

When we are trying to shift a problematic pattern, a good technique is to break down exactly how we got so good at it in the first place. This can seem kind of backwards; it is in fact a type of paradoxical strategy. When first trying this, it may seem like I'm not doing anything special, I just end up stressed out and tired a lot. But the truth is, I am making all kinds of choices inside along the way. And it's useful to shine a light on those internal choices and dynamics.

Much of what we do internally as we get stressed out and stay that way goes unnoticed. But to finally break cycles of stress and reach lasting calm, it's vital to know what we're already doing so well when we are feeling stressed. As we get a better handle on what is happening internally, we gain a new understanding and greater control. It's then easier to shift those patterns and create calm.

We will be unpacking these often-unnoticed patterns by identifying Nine Stress Secrets as we go along in the book. These Nine Stress Secrets are the sometimes sneaky internal dynamics that support and even create more stress.

Naming these Stress Secrets will help crack the code of what may be going on inside when you feel stressed out. As you notice which of the Stress Secrets apply to you, you will more easily be able to stop the stress-creating patterns. It will then be simpler to make new internal choices that create lasting calm and greater ease in your life.

Why "Conscious Calm?"

Why is this book titled "Conscious Calm?" Why don't we just focus on finding effective ways to get calm, and let that be good enough?

Because so many of the inside dynamics of stress are kind of a mystery to many people, it's common for people to feel stressed out without knowing fully how they got there. It can feel like you randomly ended up stressed out and worried. You didn't mean to get here, and may not be quite sure how it got so bad. It can happen on a kind of autopilot, without your knowing the turns in the road that you took to end up in such a worried, stressed-out place.

On the other hand, it's not very likely that you will accidentally, randomly end up feeling calm and centered. People don't often find themselves in a state of calm and ease out of the blue when they have felt stressed out and worried for a while. Finding calm and greater centeredness requires awareness, especially when starting out in a more stressed or worried state.

In fact, greater awareness or consciousness about what we are doing internally and what internal moves are better for us does lead to a deeper, more lasting state of calm. In that way, Conscious Calm is both the path and the destination.

There are ways to strengthen Conscious Calm and walk that path more effectively. So in addition to exploring Stress Secrets to understand how we got so good at stress, we will also reveal Nine Keys to Conscious Calm. These internal Keys can unlock the doors to calm and happiness for you. Using these Keys to Conscious Calm and the exercises and tools that go with them will help you live your life with greater ease. Then calm can become the more familiar home territory, instead of stress and worry.

Try This:

Think about the times of day when you tend to feel the most stressed or find yourself worrying the most. What is that stress and worry about if you consider external pressures? What is going on inside that might be adding to the stress?

How would you prefer to feel when those external challenges come up?

See if you can jot down a few responses to these questions; they will help guide you as you continue to read. You will know more specifically when you tend to feel more stressed, which will help you know when to try some of the Conscious Calm tools we will discuss. And you will know more exactly how you would like to feel instead, which can help you reach that goal more effectively.

REMINDER!

If you have not yet downloaded your complimentary *Try This Action Steps*, this would be a good time!

Visit http://consciouscalm.com/trythis and download your copy right now if you haven't yet.

2

Autopilot and Motor Mind

Why Just Thinking About Being Calmer Can't Work For Long

Perhaps you have considered stress-reduction tips and techniques in the past. Some people do try to get to the gym more often, or drink more water, or rearrange their To-Do list. As we've discussed, these things have their place; they can be very helpful.

But here we are looking at deeper, longer-lasting methods to getting a handle on stress. We are focusing on the INSIDE engines that function as deeper creators of stress and worry.

So while it's natural to look at outside stressors in our life and try to get some of those outside things under our control, that's not where all of the action is. What's true of many stressed-out people is that they have some internal patterns that they are often not aware of. These patterns can actually create even more stress, and can leave people feeling that their life is exhausting, out of control, and unfulfilling.

Part of this can start with an old habit of looking outside of ourselves for answers and information. We are trained to do this from childhood; in school we were trained to believe that textbooks and standardized tests had all the right answers.

Later we are trained to look at media, institutions of government, and religion as the holders of correct information and answers. It becomes a habit to look outside of ourselves for information. This can easily become overwhelming, as there is more information available now than at any other time in the planet's history.

Naturally, then, most of us have it ingrained to look outside of ourselves when we have a problem or when something goes wrong. This can lead to a common belief when people are stressed out. The unrecognized and unspoken belief goes something like this:

"I have stress at work and at home with my boss and with my partner. Those causes of stress are outside of me. And my outside problems are not just *contributing* to my stress and worry; they are the only *causes* of my stress and worry."

When people operate from this belief they are looking purely outside. From within that world view, other people or events are the only causes of stress.

When someone holds that world view tightly, she will do one of two things. She will tend to over-focus on trying to control the outside stress to relieve the stress and worry, or she will blame the outside stressors for how she feels. Either way, she may be left feeling more out of control and like more like a victim than a powerful person in her own life.

When outside stress seems to be the *only* cause of stress, and when people lack knowledge or awareness of some of their internal dynamics, they are in double trouble. These stressed-out people miss underlying contributions —or even causes—of high stress and worry in their life.

That's a mistake that people pay for with their peace of mind, and sometimes their health.

When we focus on outside problems as the only cause of stress, we tend to hand over our personal power to problems *out there*. We look outside for the problems as well as the solutions. If the things outside don't change, we feel even *more* powerless and out of control. Everything ends up feeling bigger than we are, or like it's never going to end.

For so many people, this is an easy and understandable mistake. First, we're trained to look outside of ourselves. Then, problems out there can be so chronic or overwhelming, it's easy to overlook where much of the additional action is. On top of that, most of us are not taught how to track or know clearly what is going on inside of ourselves, either mentally or emotionally.

So for many of us, it feels natural to believe, "If the outside stuff only got resolved, *then* I'd feel calmer, *then* I'd be able to relax." And when those outside challenges aren't solved yet, our high stress and worry continue, or even get worse.

What is overlooked in all of this attention to the outside problems is the *internal* action. And it's the internal action that often is keeping the engines of stress and worry running in overdrive.

This leads us to the first Stress Secret we want to name and consider:

Stress Secret #1:
The underlying engine that can drive us to feel
even more stressed out and worried is INSIDE of
us, not outside of us.

∞∞

What does that mean? If you're thinking right now, "OK, this is clearly crazy. My stress DOES start from out there, you should hear my boss, or see my schedule, or…!"

That's understandable; this can be a strange idea for some. It may not feel comfortable at first to look inward at stress that feels 100% like it's coming from Out There.

However, this shift in perspective holds the first key to greater calm and control. This is the start to reaching true personal power, internal control, and Conscious Calm.

Conscious Calm Key #1:
Learning to see clearly what is happening
INSIDE can give you more power over stress and
worry than you've ever had.

From Outside to Inside

So let's unpack Stress Secret #1 first—this idea that an underlying engine of ongoing stress and worry is actually INSIDE.

As an example, let's say that one major cause of feeling stressed out is a stressful job, plus having a lot of tasks and responsibilities at home. These are common, everyday situations for many people. They are, in fact, outside-of-me kinds of challenges.

It sure can seem like those problems are *only* Out There.

It sure can seem like if those problems Out There all magically disappeared one fine morning, *then* I'd be relaxed and calm.

It sure feels like it's *those problems out there* that are stressing me out and making me worry all day and half the night.

But here's the deeper reality of what's going on, and the information given to us by the first Key to Conscious Calm:

While the problems and challenges do exist out there, it's *what you tell yourself about those problems all day long*, and the choices you make INSIDE your mind, that help drive the underlying engines of feeling stressed out and worried.

What does this mean?

This internal engine of stress and worry has two parts.

One is: Where we choose to put our attention from moment to moment.

The other is: How we talk to ourselves about that focus of our attention all day long, plus the meaning we make from that self-talk.

The Hidden Power of Self-Talk

Let's look first at the power of self-talk in our internal experience. I am not referring to affirmations; those can be useful, but also do not work for many people. What I mean here is the ongoing self-talk that goes on all day, and often into the night. Mostly, we are not even aware of what we are telling ourselves about our life and ourselves.

Our self-talk combines with our habits of attention—where we choose to put our attention and focus. Our attention usually is *not* on that stream of thinking, which affects us in ways we do not even realize.

This internal thought stream of loosely-linked stories, judgments, and conclusions can bring on strong, negative emotions. These emotions produce additional stress hormones in the body, and trigger a host of other biochemical changes that leave us feeling lousy, more stressed, and tired.

This complex internal chain of thinking and feeling is entirely an "inside job."

Most of us are really good at this. Many of us are true masters of internal stress creation. Usually we don't even notice that we're doing such a good job of creating and sustaining stress and negative feelings. It goes on without our awareness, as if it's happening all by itself.

This internal stress creation comes in part from what I call internal Autopilot. We're so accustomed to this chain of thoughts and feelings that we don't even notice it's going on; it keeps running as if on its own. We don't even notice or realize the choices we make in this dynamic as it's happening.

Our thoughts take off in one direction, and we automatically jump on that train of thought and ride it, sometimes for hours. When there is strong emotion connected to that thought stream, we tell ourselves things that make us feel angry, or guilty, or not good enough.

Usually we don't even notice that we've jumped on the train, and at times it may take hours for that particular train of thought to stop or switch to another track.

Have you ever given a real listen to the internal thought stream that comes from Autopilot thinking? Here's a common example:

"I never should have let him talk to me that way. I can't believe what a moron he is. He probably thinks I'm stupid, but HE'S stupid. If I had any guts at all I'd tell him off in front of everyone, but I'd get fired, and then I wouldn't even have a job. And I still haven't paid off that credit card, and the car insurance is due, and when are we ever going to get a vacation from all this? The neighbors just got back from their vacation in Vegas, it's been years since I've been able to do something like that, it sure isn't going to happen this year. I'll never get a break, I hate this."

Many of us can go on like this for hours at a time. I call this automatic habit of intense self-talk the Thought Torrent, when we don't notice we've headed into an internal stream of thought, which gains more and more force as we add thoughts and feelings to the internal stories.

The Thought Torrent can leave us even more stressed and tired by the end of the day. And it can seem like we got that tired and drained out of nowhere. Being on Autopilot for hours with an intense Thought Torrent is more exhausting than we may know. This internal dynamic saps our strength, drains us of our natural energy, and can leave us unhappy without really knowing why.

Information Overload and Motor Mind

Another reality that feeds the Thought Torrent and contributes to our stress and worry is the vast amount of information that's available to us. It's been estimated that one daily issue of the New York Times contains more information than someone in the 1600s would have encountered in a lifetime.[7] We are exposed to much more information than we can process. We're not built for that kind of information overload, or for the popular activity of multi-tasking and pretending that's more productive (it's not[8]).

All of this information coming at us, and our habit of over-thinking, feeds Thought Torrent. The endless gathering of bits of information, our thinking so much and not being able to turn off our thoughts when we want to, is part of what I call Motor Mind.

Motor Mind seems to have its own revved-up engine, and no apparent fuel source. Motor Mind seems to have discovered the secret to renewable energy; it seems to never run out of fuel and stop on its own.

Motor Mind can go on and on internally without our even noticing that it's happening—it can be an underlying chatter that just seems normal.

The content of Motor Mind can include seemingly important information, ongoing internal commentary, or judgments about others or ourselves. It also can include more intense cascades of Thought Torrent when it really gets going and connects with strong emotion.

It can be an interesting and even astonishing experiment to just track your thoughts for a while, and see what's going on in there.

I've asked Counseling graduate students to take five minutes to write down every single thought that arises, to help them notice what they are up against when they are trying to listen well to a client. Many students finish with two or three pages of random-sounding, loosely connected, not-too-interesting sentences. They then realize that this is the mainly nonsense content of their mind all day long!

This endless, random thinking is something that has been addressed by counselors of different stripes, as well as by many spiritual traditions over the centuries.

In modern life in general, this endless, random thinking is rarely discussed. We act as if thinking without ceasing is normal. And what's worse, it can seem as if any random thought that floats through our mind must be true, just because we are thinking it.

We get ourselves into all kinds of trouble believing the thoughts that just happen to float up.

Have you seen the bumper sticker: "Don't believe everything you think"? This holds a helpful guiding tip. Our thoughts are hugely biased by past habits, emotions, judgments, experiences, and beliefs.

We are not supposed to be thinking machines on overdrive. We are not wired as human beings to spend our life with endless Thought Torrents and Motor Mind running the show.

Motor Mind explains one of the underlying, internal engines of stress and worry. When Motor Mind is on Autopilot creating an endless thought stream, we can't help but end up stressed, worried, and exhausted.

And when Motor Mind gets going with strong emotion, with a Thought Torrent of stories about the stressful things out there ruining your life, it's easy to miss how the internal action is actually creating MORE stress and worry, not less.

Stress Secret #2 points a way out of this trap:

Stress Secret #2:

We make internal choices all day long with our
thoughts, feelings, and attention, which can add
to our stress and worry.

In a way, that's the bad news: many of us spend all day long
making internal choices (that may not even feel like choices) that
actually fuel and amplify our stress and worry.

It may seem like more bad news that many of us are experts at
keeping this going all day long, usually without noticing that it's
happening.

But there is good news in all of these dynamics, and it's one of the
skills available to you as a human being:

Conscious Calm Key #2

We have the built-in capacity to use our power
of inner choice. We can choose a path to greater
calm.

The Power of Inner Choice

The truth is that we do make a choice every time we jump on a
train of thought. We are making choices every time we allow Motor
Mind to run on overdrive for hours. We are the ones making the
internal choices to give the mental train of thought both mental and
emotional fuel it as it careens on.

Recognizing that these are choices can be challenging. These internal moves into Motor Mind and Autopilot can be such deep internal habits that for many people, they don't feel like choices at all.

But considering the reality that we do have a choice from moment to moment is one key to Conscious Calm. And it can be liberating.

Once we realize how much power we actually have internally, we can begin to do something different. Using this knowledge to practice making new choices, we begin to invite true power, calm, and greater control into our life.

Because we are the ones who turn on Motor Mind, rev it up, and keep it running on overdrive without even noticing, we also can learn to stop it. We can learn to shift the habit of being on internal Autopilot, and we can learn to turn Motor Mind off, by consciously hitting the pause button on Motor Mind.

Try This:

Get a piece of paper and pen and some kind of timer. Set the timer for five minutes.

Then just begin writing every single thought that comes up in your mind. Whatever it is, just write it down. It can be "I don't know what to write," "This is stupid," "When is lunch?" or whatever. Just keep putting your attention on your thoughts, and writing down whatever comes.

At the end of the time, read over what you've written. What do you notice? Does it sound familiar? Unique? More habitual?

3

Hit the Pause Button on Motor Mind

Reclaiming Inner Choice

For many people it can seem strange to consider having real inner choice and control over a seemingly mighty force like Motor Mind.

Motor Mind can feel like it has a mind of its own, so to speak. I have heard countless people talk about what their mind recently was doing *to* them as if their mind was not a part *of* them. Many stressed people describe common experiences like this:

"I got to sleep, but I woke up at 2:00 a.m. and my mind got going, and it wouldn't stop. I couldn't get back to sleep until after 4:00!"

That sure is what it can feel like in the middle of the night when we're stressed out and Motor Mind is going strong. But notice that this person is talking about his mind as if it's a neighbor's dog barking, waking him up at 2:00 a.m. and not letting him sleep.

Of course this is a common way of speaking, and everyone will know what the man means.

But this language also points to how we sometimes disempower ourselves. The way this person describes his mind interrupting his sleep, it's as if he believes his mind and thoughts are something outside of himself. It's a statement made as if he thinks he had no choice or control in the matter until the mind itself decided to stop, or until exhaustion set in despite the mind's revved up Autopilot activity.

The reality is, of course, that this dynamic is not something outside of us. When we wake up at 2:00 a.m. and our "mind gets going and won't stop," what is really happening?

The obvious truth is that thinking is happening, and we are doing the thinking. We are also the ones who are believing the thoughts that come up, and allowing Autopilot to run much of our internal show.

We're actually in charge in many ways; it just doesn't feel that way. That's because without noticing it, we have handed the controls over to our internal Autopilot, and feel at the mercy of our mind.

A more accurate description of the example above would be something like this:

"I woke up at 2:00 a.m. and started thinking. I believed the thoughts that arose and added to them with a dramatic story line. Then I added emotional energy and more thoughts to the story. My body tensed up from all of this, and I kept worrying and getting more tense until 4:00 a.m., when I was exhausted and finally fell asleep despite it all."

We *do* have a lot of choice in the matter from moment to moment when our mind "gets going and doesn't stop." But for so many of us, Autopilot has become a deep habit, and even a way of life.

Especially for many stressed-out people, a common pattern develops. Stressed-out people often rev up Motor Mind on Autopilot and follow the Thought Torrent it generates, adding strong emotions that fuel the worried and tension-filled thoughts into even greater intensity.

This pattern actually generates *more* stress. It can happen during the day, and often comes up at night for many stressed and worried people. The cycle can go on and on for hours until sleep comes out of exhaustion. Tense or anxiety-ridden dreams might then wake them up again, or leave them tired and feeling spent in the morning, still needing rest.

So what is the alternative? How do we harness the power of our inner choice muscles? How do we start to weaken this deep pattern of Autopilot and hit the pause button on Motor Mind?

The answer lies in our power of attention.

The Hidden Power of Attention

Where we put our attention can determine how in- or out-of-control we feel.

Where we choose to focus our attention determines where we add our mental and emotional energy. And that influences how we experience our life.

This is one of the explanations of the seeming power of Motor Mind, and another aspect of how inner stress creation works.

∞◇

Stress Secret #3
Choosing to put your attention on worry-filled
thoughts and adding energy to them is a great
way to fuel Motor Mind and generate lots of
stress.

∞◇

We keep Motor Mind in motion through an automatic or unconscious choice to listen to what our thoughts happen to be saying on Autopilot. We put enough attention on the thoughts to believe them, but not enough to notice what we are doing with our attention or thoughts.

We don't recognize that we're paying enough attention to the internal story line to believe it and adding our energy to it, fueling Motor Mind's intensity. Then we don't notice that Motor Mind has fully revved up and taken off again. And we often don't notice that we have gotten even more tense or upset or stressed as a result of all this inner action.

Bringing our attention to Motor Mind itself, actually noticing that it has started up again, begins to change this repetitive, draining process.

Conscious Calm Key #3:
Bringing our attention to what Motor Mind is
doing awakens our power of inner choice.

Once I have noticed that Motor Mind is off and running again, I am putting my attention on the dynamic as it happens. I am more aware of what's going on inside. I am bringing both *attention* and *awareness* to the process of my mind—to the choices I made without noticing, and their effects.

Without both *attention* and *awareness*, we are setting ourselves up for allowing Autopilot to run the internal show. When we allow Autopilot to run without our attention or awareness, we set ourselves up for the continuing creation of more stress and worry.

This helps explain why we humans are so good at creating and maintaining high levels of stress. Many of us are used to listening to internal Autopilot in much of our life. When we are on Autopilot, we keep up the mental chatter and emotional stories that stress us out without noticing we are doing this to ourselves. In that way, Autopilot actually supports Motor Mind.

Stress Secret #4
Motor Mind is strengthened when we are on Autopilot and remain unaware or unconscious.

However, since we *do* have the power of inner choice, we can break this pattern down. This begins with bringing both attention and awareness into the picture.

Activating and using your attention and awareness helps break the automatic patterns of Motor Mind. It's the most effective way to hit the pause button on Motor Mind's ceaseless activity.

Using your awareness and attention well is one of the most important internal muscles and skill sets you can develop in your life.

~~~~~~~~~~~~~~~~~~~~~~~~~~~~

Conscious Calm Key #4

Amplifying our internal Attention and Awareness
can change EVERYTHING.

~~~~~~~~~~~~~~~~~~~~~~~~~~~~

The most successful people have one thing in common: they have developed at least some mastery of both attention and awareness.

Skillful use of attention and awareness brings inner choice into the picture. Using our inner choice, we can better direct our life and experiences from the inside. We strengthen our inner control. We no longer need to be buffeted about so much internally by circumstances outside of us, or by our old habits of Autopilot on the inside. We harness our power of choice to stop generating stress, and to create more of the internal experiences we actually want.

Learning to use attention, awareness, and inner choice paves the way for our successful journey toward Conscious Calm and greater personal power.

Attention and Awareness – What's the Difference?

Attention and awareness are not the same thing, although they are related. It is useful to be clear on what they are and how they work.

Attention is one of the functions of our cognitive or thinking mind. It's a mechanism of our thinking capacity. We put attention here, or we put our attention there; it's similar to moving a pointer or a spotlight onto something.

One of the Old English definitions of attention is "watchful." Attention has to do with observing or noticing. With attention, we can observe that Motor Mind has begun its racing with some engaging or dramatic story line.

While *attention* is the mechanism that directs our mind to something, *awareness* is more of a state.

Awareness has to do with having knowledge or realization about something. It is about being conscious of what we have directed our mind to focus on.

When we focus on something with our attention, we can use our awareness and knowledge of what is happening. We then can make deliberate choices about what we're focusing on. Attention and awareness bring choice. Do we want to keep our attention there, or would it be helpful to move it somewhere else? What would be most useful? What do we want at the moment?

I believe attention and awareness are two of the least-understood features of our human makeup. We use attention all the time, but often in an Autopilot way. That's really partial attention without conscious choice. Many people are led by whatever random thing catches their attention.

A new e-mail popped up in my inbox? I'm there! Updates on social media? I'm checking them! A judgmental thought going through my mind about that person at work? I'm all over it, elaborating it into a story that seems to make me feel better.

This superficial jumping around with our attention is actually a big waste of our energy. Many of us have a habit of skimming on the surface of whatever catches our attention in the moment, and then hopping over to the next thing.

Both the media and entertainment industries thrive on this, as does much of the "news." "What's new? What's next?" the mind wants to know, as it stays hungry for more and more new things to catch its attention for a few moments.

This is not a recipe for full, rich living, for real productivity, or for peace of mind.

Our human mind is infinitely more powerful than this internal jumping bean. We are all so much greater than how we show up when we are on Autopilot. But if we simply accept or put up with Autopilot, it can never lead us to calm, happiness, or the fulfillment of our great potential.

When we recognize the power of attention and awareness, we no longer have to be caught up in whatever shows up externally or internally. We don't need to jump automatically at whatever happens to enter our field of attention, from inside *or* outside.

We can strengthen our muscles of inner choice, and proactively, deliberately choose where we put our attention much more of the time.

This process begins by our becoming more aware of the internal habits and patterns we already have in place. When we catch ourselves in these old internal habits, we can make a more informed choice that strengthens calm instead of creating stress.

Attention! Choice Points are Everywhere!

The power of Autopilot lies in its running Motor Mind without our full awareness or our attention. Without awareness, we fuel Motor Mind with our energy.

It's kind of like sleepwalking. A lot may be going on, but it's not in our consciousness; we miss all the action.

Even then, we *are* making choices and using our attention, we're just doing it without conscious awareness. This is what feeds Motor Mind the juice to keep on running. As Stress Secret #4 reminds us, the more we are on Autopilot, the more we are likely to be strengthening Motor Mind.

The way out of the Motor Mind trap is to heighten our awareness of what we are doing in our mind – to bring our awareness and our attention to the inner choices we are making.

Because awareness has to do with knowledge and consciousness, awareness is very powerful. Conscious Calm Key #4 holds a deep truth: greater awareness and attention can change everything about our life in positive, potent ways.

Simply knowing more about Motor Mind and recognizing it can weaken old patterns. Once something is in our awareness and we have recognized a pattern in ourselves, if we continue adding our awareness to it, the pattern *has* to lose strength.

So as we amplify our awareness and strengthen our inner choice muscles, Autopilot and Motor Mind both begin to weaken. They have to. Autopilot and Motor Mind have no chance against increased awareness and proactive attention.

Part of the power of this shift is in what occurs when we bring more attention and awareness to our internal stress creation.

When we decide to end the cycles of Motor Mind and Autopilot and develop Conscious Calm, we also bring our intention into the mix. Adding our intention and decision with emotional strength behind it helps us return to awareness over and over again. Then when Motor Mind begins to run, we notice it sooner and can activate inner choice more quickly.

For example, it's common to head into Autopilot and Motor Mind when something suddenly goes wrong.

If I lock my keys in the car when I need to be somewhere in twenty minutes, I may begin to tell myself stories about how this is going to ruin my day.

If I keep this story going without noticing, I am pretty likely to end up more worked up and stressed. I am feeding Motor Mind. If I keep the story going about how my day was ruined by locking the keys in the car, my mood may sour, my decision-making won't be as sharp, and I might even make things worse.

But because I have decided to practice greater awareness and attention, I can notice sooner that this is another choice point in my day. I notice more quickly that Motor Mind is starting up. When I become aware of my unconscious choice of attention, I can proactively choose again.

Now I can choose to put my attention back on present time. I can solve how to get my car unlocked and my keys back in my hand. I can choose to just figure it out and adjust so I can go on with my day. I can call people to let them know I'll be a little late. I might remember that I put a spare key in a magnet box under the wheel rim. I can regain my sense of humor about the whole thing.

I'm no longer feeding Motor Mind. I'm not wasting my internal energy on unrecognized stress creation. I have clearer thinking and more energy to be flexible and proactive about what happened, instead of letting the sudden setback influence my mood and behavior for hours.

As soon as I have recognized or brought awareness to what I am doing internally, that hits the pause button on Motor Mind. When we become more aware that the Motor Mind cycle is happening again, we can break the spell. Our awareness makes all the difference.

Once we are more aware of what's going on, we can exercise the power of inner choice. We can choose to say out loud, "Stop!" to help break the internal trance. That's another good way to put the brakes on Motor Mind.

Once we've notice Motor Mind has revved up again, we can laugh at the repetitive nature of our mind. Or we can change internal channels and move our focus to something pleasant. Or we can bring our attention to something we are grateful for.

We have thousands of these internal choice points every day.

Each time we practice bringing our awareness to what is happening inside, it helps strengthen our inner choice muscles. We can notice that the mind has started up again on a path that is draining and unhelpful. We can hit the pause button on Motor Mind by the strength of our awareness and the power of our inner choice.

With our attention and awareness we stop the sleepy trance of Autopilot and the frantic pace of Motor Mind. We break the pattern of internal stress creation. Then we can choose where we actually want to put our attention and awareness instead.

Try This:

Think about and jot down your responses to these two questions:

When do you tend to most easily go into Autopilot and run Motor Mind?

What would be the most powerful time of day for you to increase your awareness and pause Motor Mind?

4

An Ally of Conscious Calm
Adding to Your Inner Tool Kit

As we learn how to amplify and strengthen our attention and awareness, it helps to have tools.

One of the best and most powerful tools in our Inner Tool Kit is actually always with us. This often-forgotten friend is one of our greatest allies on the path to Conscious Calm: our breath.

If we're walking the planet, we are breathing all the time, of course. But as in so much of our life, we usually breathe automatically, without attention or awareness on the breath.

Most people rarely breathe with attention. Perhaps they suddenly become more aware when they get out of breath if they are moving fast, or if a cold, allergies, or asthma prevent smooth and easy breathing. Otherwise, for most people, breathing usually goes on more or less automatically, all day long.

However, when we breathe automatically and without awareness, we miss out on the breath's full potential. Our breath is one of our best partners for increasing calm, and is a potent tool for gaining greater inner choice and control.

To take advantage of this excellent tool that is always available to us, we need to practice bringing our attention and our awareness to the breath.

Activating Breath for Conscious Calm

To activate the breath as your own inner tool for calm, try shifting your attention to your breath right this minute.

With your attention fully on your breathing, bring in your awareness as well, and notice what your breath is like. Don't change how you are breathing; just breathe normally. Observe what the quality of your breath is at the moment. Is your breath slow or fast? Does your breath feel smooth or choppy? Relaxed, or with some holding or tightness?

Next, notice how far down into your body your breath goes. Where does your breath stop before turning around and coming back out of your lungs? Does your breath go down to your heart area? Maybe down as far as your lower ribs? All the way down to your stomach?

A normal, healthy breath is supposed to go all the way into our stomach area. And our stomach should come OUT as we breathe IN, like a healthy baby breathes.

You've seen a healthy baby breathe when she's lying on her back? Every breath the baby takes, her stomach fills up like a little balloon. You can see her tummy go up and down with every breath in and every breath out.

THAT is what a healthy, normal breath looks like—for any of us! We are supposed to breathe fully and deeply, with our breath reaching all the way down to the abdomen. Our breath should engage the diaphragm and move the abdominal area out before turning around and leaving the lungs, bringing the stomach area back in again.

Most stressed-out people do not breathe fully down into their stomach.; a chest breath is much more common for them. In fact, chest breathing has become the new normal for many people.

Even *backward* breathing occurs among some stressed-out people. People who breathe "backward" hold IN their stomachs as they breathe IN; this is exactly the reverse of a healthy, normal breath.

Backward breathing is a very tense holding of the breath. Like other forms of stress breathing, over time it can support stress and worry, and actually prevent the experiences of relaxation and calm.

Stress Secret #5
Chest breathing and holding the breath help
create stress and worry. Tight breathing can
support Autopilot and sustain Motor Mind.

Chest breathing and tight or held breath is what I call "stress breathing." Stress breathing paves the way for the creation of even more tension, stress, and worry.

When we bring our attention and awareness to our breath, we reactivate the breath as a tool of inner choice and control. We reclaim the breath as an ally and ever-present support in our journey toward greater ease and Conscious Calm.

~~~~~~~~~~~~~~~~~~~~~~~~~~

Conscious Calm Key #5
Choosing to put our attention on our breath and
becoming aware of its power pave the path to
Conscious Calm.

~~~~~~~~~~~~~~~~~~~~~~~~~~

When we choose to bring both awareness and attention to our breath, we activate the natural power of breath in two important ways.

First, our breath can trigger helpful changes in our body's biochemistry and internal network of communication, creating greater calm and relaxation throughout the body.

Second, focusing on the breath in specific ways can strengthen our internal muscles of inner choice and control, helping us develop true personal power.

The Power of Breath for the Body

When we put our attention on our breath and lengthen it with awareness, we return to breathing the way our body is designed to breathe. Deeper and slower breathing naturally feels more relaxing. It rebalances the CO_2 and oxygen levels in the body, allowing the brain and the rest of the body to be nourished sufficiently with oxygen.

Another major reason deeper breath is so powerful is its effects on the vagus nerve.

The vagus nerve is one of the body's central nerves. It is the major nerve that starts in the brain stem and winds all the way down through the throat area, the heart area, the stomach, and the rest of the digestive tract. It is one of the major ways our parasympathetic nervous system is controlled.

This part of our nervous system is outside of our conscious awareness and regulates our heartbeat, digestion, immune system, and some muscle movement, among other things.

During shallow, quick chest breathing, we are breathing like someone who is experiencing the well-known "fight-or-flight" response.

The fight-or-flight response is a body mechanism that developed long ago, when humans had to run from threatening wild animals on a regular basis. In fight-or-flight mode, stress hormones increase, our heart rate gets faster, and the entire body prepares to either run or fight for its survival.

In modern times, we're typically not running from a wild animal; we're not physically running from anything. We usually are activated into "fight-or-flight" either by something outside of us that makes us scared or nervous, or by thoughts inside that run a story of desperation or crisis. Our body responds with the appropriate stress hormones, including adrenaline that gets us ready to run fast, or fight for our life.

The trouble is that we don't use all of those stress hormones and an activated body to sprint away to safety. We're usually sitting in a chair, lying in a bed, or walking or driving when we become intense and over stimulated. Instead of using that energy immediately, we often stay relatively still. The fight or flight response continues, leaving our body in a heightened, tension-filled state without a chance to use all of that energy and then relax again.

Getting into fight-or-flight mode on a regular basis causes stress hormones to course through the body, leaving the entire body acting as if there is a crisis. Over time, getting into this state regularly can damage the body and even cause illness. [9, 10, 11]

Much of this internal communication about activating the body into high gear or calming it down is run through our nervous system and our biochemistry. The communication about calming down the body is in part achieved by the vagus nerve. The good news is that even though the vagus nerve runs processes outside of our awareness, like heart rate and digestion, we can influence the information the vagus nerve sends through the body and back to the brain.[12]

When we connect with our breath through awareness and attention, and choose to lengthen our breath and slow it down, the vagus nerve begins important communication with the body and brain. The vagus nerve begins to pass along the information that the current moment is actually safe. No wild animals are about to pounce, and at the moment we are okay.

Slower, deeper breathing activates our diaphragm. This prompts the vagus nerve to communicate that the stress hormones and increased blood flow are not needed, and that the body can move into rest and relaxation again.[13]

When we take eight to ten slower, deeper breaths, we give the vagus nerve time to send this calming signal to all of the surrounding nerves up and down our major organs. It gives the vagus nerve the chance to signal to the brain and the entire autonomic nervous system the message that "All is safe right now." This helps relax the fight-or-flight response and engage the "relaxation response" throughout the body. Our entire system gets the message that it is safe in the moment, and the body becomes calmer and more relaxed.

Using breath as a vehicle for calming the body, we can rely on the vagus nerve to help spread the internal good news that this moment, right now, is safe. Instead of creating stress hormones and readying the body to run for its life, we support ourselves in bringing the body to a more relaxed state.

Breathing slowly with attention on the breath, and with awareness of how the breath can be used, we begin to stand down the state of high alert. This allows more calming biochemistry to move through the body. We let ourselves know in an experiential way that right in this moment, there is no immediate danger; we are safe, and can breathe easy.

Breath as a Vehicle for Conscious Calm

In addition to calming the physical body by bringing our attention and awareness to breath, we also can use the breath as a transformative tool in our path toward Conscious Calm.

When we bring attention to our breath and stop our Autopilot breathing, it can short-circuit other Autopilot activity as well. We then are in a position to put our inner choice muscles to use and strengthen our inner control.

Breathing with tight breath not only keeps the body tense and ready for fight-or-flight, it also serves Motor Mind. When we breathe without full awareness and with tight stress breathing, we are much more likely to be on mental Autopilot. In Autopilot, without enough attention or awareness, we are more likely to bring on Motor Mind, and Motor Mind is almost always revved up about the past or about the future.

You are probably familiar with past and future thinking. Some people tend to do it a lot, usually in Autopilot mode.

Past thinking involves replaying something that already happened. This can include worrying that something went wrong with a conversation or event, going over how we were misunderstood or hurt, or feeling regret, guilt, or shame about something we did, or think we did, or fear we may have done...

"I should have… I shouldn't have…"

"He should have…she shouldn't have…"

"I can't believe that I… I can't believe that she…"

"Why did I ever…?…Why didn't they…?"

It can go on and on. Have you ever noticed how much it saps your energy when Motor Mind gets going about the past? That's partly because our body functions best when it is giving us information about the space and time we are living in right now: the present.

When we allow Motor Mind to run on about past events for hours or days, and we don't even notice we are doing it, we drain ourselves—in part, because we are feeding huge amounts of our present energy into past memories. It's a disconnect that can cost us our energy and our wellbeing, and can leave us stressed out and tired.

Along with spinning its wheels about the past, Motor Mind also loves to grab onto stories about the future. When we're in Autopilot, we can stay with these stories for hours or days on end.

Motor Mind revved up about the future often includes "what if" thinking:

"What if I can't do it?"

"What if I screw it up?"

"What if they see me screw it up?"

"What if I don't get that job?"

"What if I *do* get the job?"

Motor Mind about the future can also include developing elaborate worst-case scenarios in our mind. Those detailed worst-case stories can start up the fight-or-flight response in our body as we get ready for the "crisis" to come.

The fact that it's in our mind and not actually happening now does not matter much to the body. Our body can have the same biochemical and other physiological responses as if the big crisis we dreamed up is actually happening right now.

That's why Motor Mind is so exhausting; we are drained in at least two important ways. Not only are we feeding our present-time energy to thoughts of past and future, we are also making the body respond as if the terrible things we envision *are* happening right now.

Both past and future Motor Mind stories can go on and on—have you noticed? While they can feel like attempts to have some kind of control, they are in fact a wonderful recipe for stress. They point to another Stress Secret that explains how and why we are so good at staying tense and stressed.

Stress Secret #6
Allowing Motor Mind to run worried stories
about the past or fearful stories about the future
are very effective ways to stay stressed out.

The Motor Mind stories that stress us out most often include what cognitive behavioral therapy calls "cognitive distortions." These are the ways we use our past habits, unhealed emotional wounds, and world views or beliefs to filter or change the facts. Creating worst-case scenarios in our mind, ("catastrophizing"), is one common example, and there are many others.

Fortunately, our breath can help us escape these mental traps and habits. Our breath can be an excellent tool for transforming these old mental patterns, because we are always and only breathing in present time.

Every time we return to bringing our attention and awareness to our breath, we can short-circuit Motor Mind. When we hit that pause button on Motor Mind, we bring ourselves back from past or future thinking. We come back to the only place and time we are living in anyway: the present.

~~~~~~~~~~~~~~~~~~~~~~~~~~~~~~~~~~

Conscious Calm Key #6
Putting attention and awareness on our breath is an effective way to stop Motor Mind activity and bring ourselves back to the present, where we actually live.

~~~~~~~~~~~~~~~~~~~~~~~~~~~~~~~~~~

When we practice using our internal choice muscles, and bringing ourselves back to the present over and over again, an interesting thing begins to occur. By *not* using our energy to fuel worried or scared thoughts of past or future, we have more energy available for the present.

We stop wasting energy on our stories about conversations from last week, on "shoulds" about the past, or on what has not yet happened in the future. We return to where we're living: right now. We have a lot more energy and clarity for our life in the present, which is the only place we have any real control and choice, anyway!

In addition to bringing us back to present time, our breath can be a vehicle for Conscious Calm in another essential way.

When we are on Autopilot with Motor Mind revved up either about the past, the future, or both, we are obviously doing a lot of thinking, whether we are noticing it fully or not. We are putting our attention and thought energy on the past or the future instead of on present time.

This creates a kind of internal disconnect.

Our body obviously lives in the present and gives us information about right now. But our mind may be off at an event ten years ago, or rehashing last week at work. Or we may be mentally jumping to an event three weeks from now, or worrying about something that may or may not happen years in the future.

The result of this is that we are more in our thoughts, more up in our head, than fully in our body. That, too, can create great stress in our system.

Our body gives us an incredible amount of information all the time. Many people, particularly stressed-out people, do not notice that information unless it comes in the form of an all-out SOS flare of physical symptoms, like a headache, or even a health crisis or illness. That then *forces* us back into the present, at least to deal with the crisis.

To transform these habits, we can return to our breath in order to come back to the body.

Breath can return us from Motor Mind fantasy to present-time reality—the only place we actually live. Breath can bring us back into the body we live in, instead of the body trying to give us data about the present while we ignore it while we focus on the stories we spin on Autopilot in our mind.

The breath, our ever-present ally, can be one of our most useful tools for bringing back calm to both body and mind.

Try This:

Ask yourself several times during the day: "Where is my breath?"

This is another way of asking yourself, "Where is my attention?"

If you weren't noticing your breath, bring awareness to your breath and choose to focus there for a few slower, deeper breaths.

You'll bring your attention away from Motor Mind activities, pull your attention from past and future thinking, and come back to your body, back to where you always have the power of choice.

See the Try This Action Steps for additional questions and tips for working with your breath.

5

Being Breaks

From Doing Back to Being

Returning to our breath during the day can invite in a new level of calm. Coming back to breath and to present time just a few times daily helps restore the body and quiet the mind. Taking slower, deeper breaths with awareness brings us back to the body, and short-circuits Autopilot mental activity about past and future. Doing this even a handful of times every day can be a big step toward feeling calmer and more in control.

When we are stressed and tense and rushing around, we are involved in Doing. Using the breath in this way moves us from Doing mode back into Being.

We may have lists of tasks To Do and a schedule of what we have To Do every day. Many people complain about not having enough time in a day to get everything Done. You may have heard the wry observation that we have morphed from Human Beings into Human Doings—and there is some truth to this.

Not only are many of us rushing around Doing tasks all day long, feeling like we can never get enough Done. That's stressful enough.

Even more subtle and more important than the *external* rushing around is our *internal* Doing all day long. The movement of thought in the mind is actually another kind of Doing. Thinking about and telling ourselves loaded stories uses our attention and our energy in ways that drain and disempower us.

How we use our thought energy has a huge effect on our overall well-being, our focus, and our effectiveness in the world. Whatever way we use thought energy, it's always a type of Doing. It's just Doing that is internal instead of external.

When we spend most of our day in Autopilot, running tense mental stories about past and future and letting Motor Mind run without awareness of what we're doing to ourselves, our energy is sapped. When we use our energy to feed these dynamics, not really noticing what we are Doing, we are supporting distraction, draining our energy, and creating even more stress for ourselves.

Motor Mind can be a deep habit. Because Motor Mind often goes on and on in Autopilot, we give little attention or awareness to what we are doing—that we are fueling internal activity and keeping it going.

This kind of internal Doing makes it difficult for us to feel relaxed or calm. When internal Doing is combined with external rushing around, being calm during the day or relaxing into sleep at night become a challenge. Continuous internal and external Doing can leave anyone feeling drained or exhausted after a while.

Realizing that we operate in Doing mode all the time, both external and internal, adds important insight into how we become stressed out and stay that way.

Stress Secret #7
Keeping up both external and internal Doing
all day long without pause is an excellent way to
promote a constant experience of stress.

High stress and endless Doing, both externally and internally, are closely related.

Doing without stopping seems normal to many people, but this endless Doing goes against our internal grain. It's not natural for human beings to Do without any pause. Sadly, between all of the external running around and the internal Motor Mind pace, we really have become Human Doings in many ways.

Modern society does not teach us much about how to be real human Beings in that sense. Not much is taught about how to Be comfortably without Doing. We actually get the opposite messages. There is plenty of support for maintaining the Human Doing way of life. Many people have a very demanding schedule and a busy life. Circumstances can be challenging and difficult. Much of entertainment and advertising is promotes ways to keep Doing— either to distract or to numb out—but not to just Be.

Lasting calm calls for the ability to pause *all* the Doing for a while and bring awareness to Being. When we recapture that inborn ability, we are brought back naturally to greater calm.

There is one simple, powerful way to break the Doing habit and return to feeling much greater calm and inner control.

~~~~~~~~~~~~~~~~~~~~

Conscious Calm Key #7
Taking a Being Break helps interrupt our internal
and external Doing habits, and allows us to
access the natural calm of Being.

~~~~~~~~~~~~~~~~~~~~

When we move toward Conscious Calm in this way, we recapture our true nature as Human Beings. For those of us who may feel more like Human Doings much of the time, taking what I call a Being Break can be helpful.

Why Take a Being Break?
A Being Break is a short pause in *both* external *and* internal Doing.

It's not enough to just sit down and stop the external hurrying. That's only part of the solution, and it is not even the most critical part. The key to a Being Break is to practice stopping the *internal* Doing, too. That puts a solid wedge into the constant Doing of both Autopilot and Motor Mind, and brings real relief.

Pausing both the outside and inside rushing around gives our mind and body a much-needed rest. Our body and mind need that rest nearly as much as the body requires food and water.

Why? Human Beings thrive on Being. It's natural. It's where we really live. We can rest from all that outer and inner Doing. We pause and connect to Being, connecting with our body and with present time, instead of jumping around internally from past to future and back again.

Taking this break in the internal and external action helps to nourish and restore both our body and our mind. We can return to the next Doing on our list feeling calmer, more refreshed, and energized.

For most stressed-out people, a Being Break is not a natural part of their day. The Doing seems to never stop. It's more usual to sprint around both physically and mentally, with Motor Mind revving up all the way to the end of the day, and even into the night.

A Being Break helps us shake up the deep internal Doing habits of Autopilot and Motor Mind. A Being Break supports us in regaining internal and external choice and control.

First we bring our awareness to our internal and external Doing and tension-filled hurrying around. Then we can use our internal choice muscles to make the decision to stop, just for a few minutes, and practice resting in Being.

How to Take a Being Break

One easy way to practice a Being Break is to use our companion and ally, the breath.

We've discussed how slower breaths with awareness can pause Motor Mind and help to short-circuit Autopilot. In part, that's because our breath, that friend that is always with us, is a natural bridge between Doing and Being.

Every time we choose to put our full attention on our breath and breathe more slowly and deeply with awareness, we are taking a short Being Break. We are stopping the external Doing, giving the mind just enough To Do internally by pointing our attention to the breaths and counting them.

Staying aware of just eight to ten breaths easily creates a link between Doing and Being. We are shifting toward the natural state of Being, at least for those few minutes.

For people who have been stressed for a while, taking a regular Being Break can be very useful. A Being Break eases the draining habit of constant Doing, and creates internal balance and control.

Deciding to take a Being Break every few hours, or even once an hour, can be a powerful practice. Some people start by programming a phone or computer alarm to remind them, which can be one helpful way to begin.

When it's time for a Being Break, stop your external Doing first. Just stop whatever you are Doing, knowing you can return to it in just a few minutes.

Sit comfortably, or lie down if it's convenient. Invite yourself to stop all outside movement of the body, and maybe take a deeper breath or two to help the body relax.

Once your body is still, bring your awareness to the *internal* movement of your mind. Bring your awareness to the thoughts that still may be running on Autopilot.

Use your full attention to notice whether the mind is still thinking. If you're stopping in the middle of a task, you can remind yourself you'll be able to pick up any important threads after the Being Break. Invite the mind to just stop its activity for a little while.

Then shift your attention and awareness fully to your breath. Breathe more slowly and a little more deeply than you were before. Connect your attention with your breath, as if it's riding the breath in and out of the lungs.

Close your eyes if that's comfortable. Then start to count ten slower, deeper breaths, allowing both the body and mind to just Be, to just rest.

After ten breaths like this, allow yourself to notice how your body feels. Does anything feel different? Notice the state of your mind. Is there any more space between thoughts? Perhaps slightly less tension in the mind?

This short pause in Doing—breathing just ten times slowly—is a valuable way to add a Being Break to your day. Posting a note in key places as a reminder to "Breathe!" can help. Reminders at home or the office—on a bathroom mirror, a refrigerator door, a computer screen, or phone—can be reminders to stop and take a Being Break for ten slower, deeper breaths.

For people who have been stressed out for a longer time, getting through even eight or ten breaths can be a challenge. Most people notice the mind goes off to the past or future. Some notice they have lost count of their breaths. Others notice they are breathing, but there is still some sneaky internal Doing going on in the form of thoughts or internal commentary: "When is this going to be over?" What's for dinner?" "Where did I leave my phone?" and so on.

If you notice any of this, just keep breathing. It's normal. It's only the mind doing what it does; that's the mind's version of Doing, and the mind is really used to it.

When the thoughts or commentaries start up, just notice the internal Doing habit, and gently bring awareness back to your breath. It will get easier, and you'll soon be feeling the relief a Being Break can bring.

Lengthening Being Breaks

Once ten breaths feel easier, and the mind stays quieter through the tenth breath, you can use the breath for a slightly longer Being Break. I usually suggest people start with just five minutes.

When you are ready to try this, set a timer for five minutes so there is no need to keep checking the time.

Use your internal choice muscles to focus on your breath. Just for five minutes, close your eyes and simply bring your attention to your breath. Become more aware of your breath, slowly coming in and going back out. You will be pausing external and internal Doing, and opening the door to Being.

You will notice the mind doing its thing sooner or later, with thoughts or commentaries coming up. Just notice this when it happens, and gently bring your attention back to your breath. Don't start another internal commentary about "What I should be doing" or "I'm not doing this right" or anything else! Just gently return to the breath for the full five minutes. You may need to bring your attention back several times in the course of five minutes. That, too, is normal.

Another Being Break technique is to use a candle to help support awareness and attention while breathing slowly and more deeply.

To try this, set a timer for five minutes. Light a candle and bring your attention to your breath and to the candle flame.

Simply watch the candle flame while breathing slowly in a relaxed manner. This gives the mind something to Do, because the flickering of the candle flame holds the mind's attention.

Some people find this easier at first than focusing on breathing with the eyes closed. The candle flame can help anchor the mind in present time, supporting a five-minute Being Break.

Once five minutes feels comfortable, you may want to extend the time to ten minutes or more.

Beyond giving the body and mind some much-needed rest from all that Doing, the relief of just Being brings its own rewards and benefits. A longer Being Break can become the anchor for greater calm, as well as a wedge into old patterns of internal and external Doing and stress creation.

Benefits of Being Breaks

Adding Being Breaks into your day will weaken the habits of both external and internal Autopilot Doing. As you practice returning to Being, you will notice the relief of not Doing all the time, both externally and internally. You will start to reap the benefits of strengthening Being within you.

With practice, Being Breaks can help you to:

- Feel more energy during the day, because you use less energy for Autopilot and Motor Mind
- Strengthen internal choice muscles and experience more control internally
- Feel more calm and centered
- Sleep better and more soundly
- Return to tasks refreshed and energized
- Deepen your concentration and focus
- Become more effective in decision-making

- Be more present to yourself; it becomes easier to know what we want or need moment to moment

- Be more present and connected to the people you care about

- Access and express creativity, which springs from Being, not Autopilot Doing

And paradoxically, stopping all Doing and taking a Being Break can help you be more efficient and get even more accomplished in less time.

Common Experiences When Starting Being Breaks

As you practice Being Breaks, you are likely to be surprised at the internal Doing you notice. Since we generally don't think of thoughts and internal storytelling as Doing, many people report surprise and even shock when they notice how much is going on in the mind all the time.

That's a good thing. You'll notice it even more as you continue practicing Being Breaks.

Over time, letting thoughts go by like clouds in a sky of Being becomes more natural. Many traditions that explore the power of Being use images like this to help people begin to witness all the Doing in their thoughts. Witnessing thoughts is more powerful than the Autopilot habit of jumping onto any train of thought that happens to go by, taking our attention and energy with it.

As you practice Being Breaks, you will also notice how much energy internal Doing uses. This may be a revelation as well. But this is also positive and helpful; you are feeling the drain of energy that internal Doing creates. You can then choose more easily to not waste that internal energy in Motor Mind activity.

As a result, you will be living more and more of your life in present time, with additional life energy available to you for living even more fully.

Try This:

Choose either the candle flame Being Break or the breathing Being Break for five minutes.

What do you notice come up in the mind?

What do you notice in your mind and body after the Being Break is over? Did it feel challenging? Like a relief? Uncomfortable at times?

Try adding a Being Break to your morning routine for just one week. How does your experience of the Being Break change over that time?

6

The Personal Power 180

Turning It Around

Using Being Breaks can help bring us back to calm. Being Breaks also help us to notice just how much energy we are using internally all day long.

Taking Being Breaks naturally amplifies both our attention and our awareness. We become better able to recognize the internal choices that are energy drains—choices that in fact weaken us.

We also begin to notice *where* we put our attention and energy. For many of us, this is a journey of becoming aware of how much attention and energy is used to focus *outside* of ourselves instead of *inside* ourselves.

Why does it matter so much whether we put our attention outside or inside?

Outward and Inward Attention

In the course of the day, everyone naturally focuses attention on some outside tasks, events, and interactions. We naturally focus on some internal realities too, like physical sensations, thoughts, pain, or pleasure, and mental activity including beliefs, conclusions, and judgments.

If you are feeling stressed, it can help to bring more awareness to where you put your attention most of the time.

Outward attention is needed, for example, when we are planning a future event, when we are engaged in a task in present time, or when we are talking with someone. That is all occurring in present time, so our energy is usually not being wasted.

However, when our outward attention moves away from present time and into speculation, energy can be drained and stress created. When our internal focus moves outward, imagining what others think about us, or wondering whether someone thinks we're okay or good enough, or if we spend time comparing ourselves to someone else and find ourselves lacking, we are putting mental focus on externals that drain our energy and weaken us. When we engage in outward mental focus like this, we lose our power instead of strengthening it.

These draining, outwardly focused thoughts use our energy to compare, justify, or head into stories of "what if."

Comparing ourselves with others may occasionally be useful. Usually, though, this practice uses story lines to either find ourselves lacking, or to feel temporarily better by judging someone else as "less than" ourselves.

Justifying goes on when we review something in the past and tell ourselves a story about why we were right, why someone else was wrong, or why it just *had* to go the way it did (when maybe that's not true).

"What if" stories are often worry-ridden thoughts about infinite future possibilities. Many of us can spend hours on "what if" scenarios.

These types of thought patterns tend to pull us into telling internal stories that rev up Motor Mind. They are rarely about something actually occurring in present time, in our lived experience.

All of these activities are an energy drain. They focus our energy outward and usually into the past or the future. We then have less energy and attention to focus on the moment and on ourselves in a more present, practical way. We end up with less capacity to notice what we are feeling, or what we need. We become less able to notice what information our body is giving us about our level of stress, our comfort, or our discomfort with circumstances. We also have less capacity to notice the effectiveness or dynamics of our interactions with other people in present time.

When we focus mostly outside and on past or future, we tend to lose energy. We especially drain ourselves when we tell Autopilot stories of what others may think of us, or wonder if others are judging us as not being good enough, smart enough, pretty or handsome enough. These are all examples of an outward focus that can leave us unnecessarily drained and disempowered.

Turning this habit around is a key part of regaining personal power as well as greater calm.

A useful technique for turning this pattern around is what I call the Personal Power 180.

Using this technique, we first can notice how much energy we drain outward in unhelpful ways. We then can turn that energy around with a U-turn (180 degrees) back to present time, reclaiming our energy, our focus, and our personal power.

Internal Vector Analysis

The Personal Power 180 technique borrows (okay, steals) the term "vector" from math and engineering. You may have heard of vectors; they are a special kind of arrow. Vectors tell us two basic things. The direction of the vector or arrow tells us in what direction energy is flowing. The length of the vector tells us how intense or strong that energy is.

So let's take an example of how to use internal vectors with our thought energy and attention as a tool for greater personal power and calm.

Let's consider Susana, who almost missed the bus to get to work. Susana is going about her day in a typical manner, feeling stressed out. She was late leaving home and had to run to catch the bus. Susana has a lot on her plate with a deadline coming up, and hasn't been sleeping very well. She is feeling out of shape, and believes she just isn't doing enough.

Susana feels frazzled and tired before she even starts her day. She rides the bus standing up, thinking and worrying like she usually does. If we imagine the vectors of Susana's thoughts and attention, what might they look like? How many of those vectors would be focused on Susana herself in present time?

Several arrows would be shooting off into the future about her work deadline, and a few more long arrows of worry about others who may be judging her. There would be longer arrows pointing toward the future, with worried thoughts about her boss or colleagues noticing that she is late again. There might be one shorter arrow pointing down to the present, with only a little of Susana's attention given to maintaining her balance during the bus ride.

With an internal vector picture like this, Susana is unlikely to feel her personal power. She is also unlikely to feel calm.

Susana's vector picture is typical of a stressed-out person in Autopilot, with a lot of her internal Doing energy flowing outward. Part of her Motor Mind activity is about the possibility of getting to the gym that week, and what her gym friends are thinking of her since she hasn't been there in over a week. A lot of her thought energy is invested in what others may (or may not!) be thinking about her.

So the majority of Susana's thought-energy vectors are heading away from herself in present time. Most of the arrows are flowing out to past, future, and others' made-up opinions or possible judgments about her. The longest arrows would not even be about work; they would be the vectors representing her thoughts and worries about others' opinions or judgments of her. This is part of an excellent recipe for stress.

Stress Secret #8

To stay really stressed out, keep your thought vectors pointing outward and toward past or future, with your internal Doing on Autopilot and Motor Mind engaged.

With a thought vector picture like Susana's, it's impossible for her to feel calm and centered, or strong and confident. There is way too much energy being spent in up-in-the-head worry, in past and future Motor Mind. That drains energy away from present time, and away from awareness of the body. Only a small amount of Susana's thought energy is on her present experience as she rides the bus. Much of her attention and energy moves outward and toward past and future, spinning stories of others' possible judgments of her.

In effect, this means Susana is giving her power to others' opinions. Little energy and power is left in present time for Susana herself. This leaves Susana stressed, more tired, and feeling insecure before she even gets to work.

To stop the flow of her energy and personal power outward to others, Susana could choose to turn these thought-energy vectors around. By practicing the Personal Power 180, Susana could bring her energy back to herself, and back to present time. She then could feel less stressed out, more calm, and more confident.

~~~~~~~~~~~~~~~~~~~~~~~~~~~

Conscious Calm Key #8
Do a Personal Power 180 to turn attention and awareness back to the present. This brings greater calm and gathers personal power instead of giving it away.

~~~~~~~~~~~~~~~~~~~~~~~~~~~

So what would the Personal Power 180 look like for Susana?

Strengthening both personal power and calm begins with increasing attention and awareness. So to start this internal U-turn, Susana begins by bringing more attention to where her thought energy is going. She checks in what direction her internal energy arrows are pointed.

By bringing her attention to the energy arrows heading outward and out of present time, Susana can notice the energy that has been flowing toward things she actually can't control because they are in the past, the future, or made up.

With attention on the internal choices she has been making without realizing it and with awareness of their effects on her, Susana instantly has more choice. She no longer has to stay stuck in her internal pattern of feeling so stressed out and insecure.

When Susana recognizes those draining outward vectors and imagines turning the outward-pointing vectors 180 degrees, she stops draining her energy outward. She stops putting energy into past and future, which she can't change or control anyway. She pulls back her thought energy from future "what ifs." She stops making up judgmental conversations with people who are not even there. She slows the flow of her energy to things that haven't even happened.

As Susana brings her attention back to the present, to her body and mind in the moment, she has more choice about what to do (or not do) now.

Susana then can choose to return fully to her ride in the bus. She can notice her surroundings, or make herself more comfortable by taking a seat instead of standing. She can take a Being Break for energy and calm before work, instead of giving in to draining, internal Doing, which weakens her and leaves her frazzled.

By noticing and turning the thought vectors around, Susana saves and strengthens her Personal Power. Instead of draining her power by giving it to others' made-up opinions and judgments, Susana returns to herself, and can become more aware of what she needs and wants.

Instead of losing energy by focusing on past and future, Susana can return to present time and make choices that can make a difference in how she feels. She can arrive at her workplace calmer and feeling more confident and in control.

The Personal Power 180 begins with amplifying attention and awareness about where our energy is going, then we choose to turn that energy around toward the present, back toward our actual lived experiences in the moment.

This process becomes simpler through using Being Breaks. When we stop external and internal Doing with Being Breaks, we notice more easily where we are putting our energy and attention. Being Breaks can help us realize when we are aiming our thought energy outward toward past, future, or made-up scary or annoying stories.

Being Breaks also strengthen our ability to turn those energy vectors around. We can then choose to practice the Personal Power 180 to bring our energy back to ourselves in present time, and make choices that strengthen us and enhance our life.

Bumps in the Road

For people who have been stressed out for a while, taking Being Breaks and exploring the internal vectors can seem difficult at first. Even a five-minute Being Break can feel like forever for some.

I have sat with many people over the years who practically ran out of the room at even the suggestion that they sit for five whole minutes to just breathe! Sitting still for five minutes can feel nearly impossible for those who are used to constant Doing and the pace of revved-up Motor Mind all day long.

When stressed-out people begin to practice Being Breaks and bring their attention back to their body, a common thing occurs. Usually sooner rather than later, they will experience some discomfort or restlessness in the body and in the mind.

Some people will just want to stop, get up, and move around, because it feels uncomfortable to just sit and Be. It's also common for those who feel this discomfort to move back into Autopilot mode, revving up commentary or stories in the mind.

Part of this is the newness of just Being, which can seem unfamiliar at first. Taking Being Breaks and noticing which way the internal energy is going can bring into sharp focus just how much we have been Doing internally. It can feel challenging to just rest both the body and the mind.

Another important part of this feeling is a natural dynamic of our body. When we finally stop external and internal Doing for a few minutes, we return to the body, and to present time. It becomes possible for us to begin to feel sensations and emotions in our body that are trying to tell us something.

Autopilot and Motor Mind, plus external rushing around, lead us to be more focused on the mental plane, and on past and future. When we reconnect with present time and with our body, suddenly a lot seems to be going on in our sensations and emotions that we may not have noticed so strongly before. We can feel discomfort or restlessness when we begin to notice and feel our body and its sensations and emotions.

What are emotions for, anyway? People have asked me this question when they start to feel discomfort in practicing just Being. To some people, emotions seem bothersome, or scary, or something that's just getting in the way of feeling better.

The truth of emotions is different. Emotions can hold a wealth of information for us about our lived experience.

We go into this in the next chapter.

Try This:

During the day, carry around a small notebook, index card, or folded piece of paper.

Ask yourself several times during the day, "Where is my attention right now?" Maybe set an hourly alarm to remind you. When you notice where your attention is and where your thoughts are going, just jot down, in a few words, what you've noticed.

At the end of the day, put a little arrow next to each note. Point the arrow outward if your attention was focused outside of yourself; point the arrow inward or toward the words if your attention was focused inward, toward yourself in present time. Then go back over the list and write next to the arrow where in time those thoughts were—"Past" or "Present" or "Future."

Notice (without judging!) how many arrows are focused outward, toward what others might be thinking/feeling. How many are inward, toward yourself?

Then notice how many arrows are heading to past or future, and how many are energizing the present.

Which of those energy vectors could you begin to turn around by activating more attention and awareness?

7

Where Emotions Come In:

What Are Feelings For, Anyway?

A Common Story of Stress

Michelle sat across from me in our first meeting and described what was going on in her life.

Michelle felt so stressed out. She couldn't turn her mind off. She found herself thinking about work more and more when she was trying to sleep. She also was waking up at night worrying about her job, and about her boyfriend, who had begun complaining that they didn't have enough time together. Michelle knew he was right, but the longer hours at work felt necessary.

Michelle said earnestly that she was trying so hard in her life, but was really stressed and worried. Her job deadlines were stressing her out, and things were busier than ever. She worried about losing her job, and possibly her boyfriend, too.

Michelle knew she had too much on her plate, but other people around her seemed to be handling their life okay, and some of them even had kids. What was wrong with her?

Michelle was in a very common situation. She was describing built-up problems and stress that she did not know how to handle. While she was stressed out and did not know what to do, she assumed something was wrong with *her* for not handling it better. The stress from outside and as well as inside felt out of control to her.

I noticed something that is common in people who are stressed out and worried: Michelle was not talking directly about her feelings. Yet, there was so much obvious emotion in her voice, her face and eyes, and in her body language.

I asked Michelle about this and what she noticed about how she felt. She answered immediately, "I'm stressed out, that's how I feel!"

Michelle's response is understandable; these days "stressed out" substitutes for a whole range of real emotions. I suggested Michelle try to put her attention on what else she could detect—where were her feelings in her body right now?

"In my body? My feelings are in my head. That's where everything is going on. There's just too much going on in my head; I think that's why I'm stressed out."

Michelle is both right and wrong here. Of course it is true that Michelle's mind is very busy and that her thoughts and worrying are part of what keep her up at night. That's a natural part of being so stressed for a long time.

But Michelle is also making a common mistake: she believes her feelings live in her head. When the buzz of stress gets that high and Motor Mind is in overdrive without pause, it sure can feel like all the action is up in the head.

This sense that "my feelings are in my head" leads Michelle and so many people in her situation to overlook a huge amount of information. She misses the data she is being given all the time by her built-in information system: her emotions. And those emotions with all their potentially valuable information are not just located up in her head.

So Where Are Our Emotions, Anyway?

Felt emotions do not simply exist "in our heads." While emotions involve thought, the main reality of emotion that is overlooked by many stressed-out people is that our emotions live in and communicate through the BODY.

Every emotion includes sensations that can be identified and felt in one or more places in the body.

For example, worry is the mental part of anxiety.

When someone is worrying a lot, he is most likely feeling at least some anxiety. If he is connected to his body and emotions, he will notice a tightening in his chest or throat, a faster heartbeat than usual, tension in his shoulders, or all of the above, and more. Those are some common physical sensations connected to the emotion of anxiety.

The catch-all phrase of being "stressed out" can include anxiety, fear, nervousness, and even panic. Stressed-out-ness always includes a range of both emotions and sensations in the body. However, stressed-out people may be unaware of the emotions and sensations showing up in their body. They may be too caught up in Autopilot Motor Mind.

What Are Emotions For?

When we are under high, chronic stress, we often are disconnected from the emotions and sensations in our body. What is the problem with missing the emotions and the sensations that go along with them? People have asked me very directly, "So what? What are emotions for, anyway?"

These are good questions. Here is the deal.

Our body is wonderfully wired to give us information all the time about our actual, lived, present-time experience. This information shows up to help us guide our life toward what feels best to us, toward what makes us happier, toward what we need and want.

Some of the information comes to us through emotion. This brilliant arrangement is frequently called our "emotional navigation system" or our "emotional guidance system."

What does that mean? We frequently are being given information about our experience through emotions. At the simplest level, emotions are supposed to come up, give us information about our experience, and then subside or go away.

When we do notice and take in what we are feeling, we are making use of our emotional guidance system. We receive information about how we are being affected, about what is and is not working for us in the moment. We then can make informed choices about what we want and need, or about how to respond. We can exercise our personal power to make the choices that best serve us and our life.

How to NOT Feel Your Emotions

Let's get back to Michelle.

I asked Michelle to take a few regular breaths with me. We observed together that her "in breath" went down only as far as the middle of her chest, to the area near her heart. Like so many people in our stressed-filled modern society, Michelle was chest breathing.

In Chapter 4 I described chest breathing and how many stressed-out people tend to breathe only as far as their chest. They have learned to tighten their stomach area, to hold their breath, and to breathe using a shallower breath into the chest.

This can become a vicious cycle. Chest breathing can cause an imbalance of oxygen and CO_2 in the body. It can create even more tension in the system. In addition, chest breathing prevents us from feeling our feelings fully.

Many children who grow up in tense or traumatic situations teach themselves to do chest breathing early on. Without being fully aware of it, they learn to tighten their stomach area, and stop themselves from fully feeling the strong or overwhelming emotions that are naturally arising in response to what they are living through.

In addition, in our society, with its mixed-up messages about what makes a beautiful body, many pre-teen and teenage girls, and boys too, start to hold in their stomachs to flatten them. When they tighten the stomach like that, they are forcing themselves to chest breathe.

They are ALSO stopping themselves from feeling all of their feelings fully.

Tightening the abdomen and shortening the breath can be a short-term strategy for not feeling strong or overwhelming emotions. However, tightening breath and pushing feelings down often becomes a habit for preventing or ignoring stronger emotions as they naturally come up.

If we get into the habit of stopping our breath from deepening into our stomach area, we upset the balance in the body and create more tension and stress for ourselves. We also miss out on receiving direct, important information about our present experiences and our life.

What Emotions Are For, Part II

We are wired to notice and feel our emotions, to recognize them as information, and to use that information to help us live fully and well.

Our body is built to breathe freely and deeply, energizing and nourishing the body with oxygen, and naturally taking in and using the information provided by our built-in emotional navigation system.

If you have learned to tighten your stomach area and to chest breathe, the good news is that it's possible to change this habit.

As we unlearn the habitual, tense holding of our breath and body and relearn how to feel more of the emotion coming up, we can be more relaxed and better informed. We have more data about what we are experiencing in our life and how it affects us—how we *feel* about it. We can know more clearly what we want or need: "Is this okay with me? What do I want right now? Do I need to speak up for myself or keep quiet?"

Then we can explore what choices we have and decide how we want to respond to the conditions and relationships in our life. We become better able to navigate our life with more personal power, integrity, and calm.

Growing Awareness of Breath and Body

Michelle reported she had been chest breathing as long as she could remember. It felt weird to her to imagine breathing all the way down into her belly. And it felt backward to have the stomach come OUT with an IN breath, because she was so used to tightening her stomach when she took a breath in.

When Michelle slowed down her breathing and lengthened it without forcing, her breath did deepen a little. Although it felt strange to her at first, with several slower, easy breaths, Michelle's "in breath" did begin to move down toward her stomach area.

After a few more slow breaths, I asked what she could feel in her body. Michelle looked at me, surprised, with slightly misty eyes, and said in a softer voice, "I'm so tired!" We noticed together that Michelle also felt some sadness, because of the stress of trying so hard for so long.

Holding our breath, running on stressed—out, frenetic energy, having galloping thoughts at night when we're supposed to get rest— all of these things take huge amounts of our energy. We are spent but still spinning, wondering why we are so tired and why we don't have more energy for living.

When Michelle deepened her breath a little, she also brought more attention to her body. By doing that, she was able to become aware of how tired she actually was. And she could notice the sadness that was there as well. This was some of the information trying to get through, sent by her Internal Guidance System.

This is no small thing. Noticing how exhausted she was helped Michelle feel the effects of striving so hard for so long. She then could think about how she could ease up a bit and get more rest. Noticing she was feeling sadness allowed her to take in on a deeper level that her current situation was making her unhappy as well as tired.

As she slowed and deepened her breathing and noticed her fatigue and sadness, Michelle was able to consider that she had options. Michelle decided to focus on getting better sleep at night as her priority, and to strategize ways to rebalance her work schedule even with looming deadlines.

Michelle then learned a few of the Being Breaks techniques and started including Being Breaks in her busy days. She began to give more attention to what the emotions and sensations in her body were trying to tell her about her life and her needs and wishes. She became more able to make choices to reduce stress externally and internally.

As Michelle practiced pausing Motor Mind, she experienced the relief of not rushing around so much both inside and outside. She was more in touch with herself and found time to connect better with her boyfriend. Michelle realized that external and internal rushing had been a choice, and that she could also choose to slow down.

What We Know About How Emotions Work

It is a common misunderstanding that our emotions live only in our brain. That idea comes, in part, from the advances in brain science over the past few decades, which hold a specific view of emotional processes.[14, 15] It also is due in part to the pharmaceutical industry's influence over doctors, psychiatrists, research, and practice.[16, 17, 18] This includes $15 billion spent (just in 2008) on "education" for doctors, which influences what information doctors receive about drugs, what is researched, and what is broadcast in the media.[19] This is a longer discussion outside of the scope of this book; if you would like to explore these issues more, see the Notes and Resources sections.

For the purpose of helping you get a better understanding of stress and worry in your life, here are some key discoveries made about how emotions function throughout the body, not just in the brain.

For complicated reasons I mentioned, large segments of Western psychology and medicine still act as if the only place emotions occur is in the brain. Brain activity is certainly involved in experiencing emotion. What is not yet discussed more commonly is the huge amount of research describing how the body processes emotions—that emotion is not only communication that happens within the neurology of the brain.

At first, scientists studied the electrical communication in our brain and nervous system solely as if the brain had lots of "wires" going through the spinal cord and body to distribute information. Only in the past few decades has the biochemical nervous system been measured and described more fully. This system works through the communication of chemical receptors and other "information molecules" throughout the entire body.[20]

One researcher who made breakthrough discoveries about this chemical information network is Dr. Candace Pert. While at Johns Hopkins, the National Institute of Mental Health, and beyond, Dr. Pert and her colleagues have measured and described this system of information molecules.

They discovered that information-carrying molecules, called peptides, were found not only in all major areas of the brain, but in fact throughout the body. In her book *Molecules of Emotion*, Dr. Pert describes her own work and that of other scientists, which shows how peptides help create a flow of information across all systems of the body. Dr. Pert makes this analogy:

"Peptides are the sheet music containing the notes, phrases, and rhythms that allow the orchestra—your body—to play as an integrated entity. And the music that results is the tone or feeling you experience subjectively as your emotions." [21]

For the past several decades, Dr. Pert and other scientists have done research that keeps showing the same conclusions: it's not simply that our brain sends signals to the rest of the body, registering emotions and other information. It's much more of a two-way information flow.

For instance, when we have a "gut feeling," this may well be due to the nerve cells and other cells in our gut lining that contain neuropeptides and receptors. It's been shown that when we are excited or angry, the movement in the gut increases, and when we are more peaceful or contented, movement decreases. In the other direction, when we eat something that "disagrees" with us or when our digestion is poor, we can become more irritable or moody.[22]

The work of Dr. Pert and others continues to demonstrate that we have a "mind-body," not a mind (or brain) separate from the body. This means, among other things, that how we feel can directly impact our health. That comes back to the health effects of being stressed out and worried over a long period of time.

With ongoing stress and worry, the body's biochemistry will include stress hormones that can prematurely age you, or cause minor as well as serious health issues, as we've mentioned. Allowing this to go on without effective intervention *from the inside* means that many people resort to taking in prescribed or other drugs *from the outside*.

The spread of pharmaceuticals to medicate unpleasant or challenging emotions is once again complex. There are times when chemical intervention can be helpful, or even needed. But part of the usual drug company advertising message is that you have no control over these emotions without external, chemical intervention. Another underlying message is, "Emotions are bad, don't listen to them. Drown them out or get rid of them. Feeling too much? Take this pill."

One danger, of course, is that we drown out or numb emotions that may inform us about our life and experiences. "Just take a pill" becomes a seemingly quick fix, a way to not feel the stronger or more challenging emotions that are labeled as a problem. Taking a pill also becomes a quick way to force the body into sleep when Motor Mind is on overdrive, or when feelings come up at the end of the day, or in the middle of the night when there are fewer distractions.

Benefits of Recognizing Our Emotions

Learning to experience more of our emotions and to work with them provides a different set of options. We gain the opportunity to stop Autopilot choices about our feelings. Becoming more skilled in hearing the body's messages, and learning to make proactive choices about them, is a path to reclaiming personal power as well as greater calm. We gain the chance to affect both how we feel and our health.

Allowing ourselves to connect with emotions more directly engages the body's natural abilities. We can make use of our Internal Guidance System and our power of choice to gain greater inner freedom, calm and personal power.

As we amplify our attention and our awareness, we learn to hear more clearly what our body is saying. This brings three huge benefits:

1. We receive information about what we actually need and want, and how the circumstances of our life are affecting us.

2. Because we have more internal information, we have a wider range of choices about what we need or want, about how to respond, and what to do. That can give us more control over present time external situations that are stressful.

3. We are better able to make proactive choices that help our body calm down. We create more of the natural breathing rhythms and biochemicals that support us in feeling calmer, less stressed, more energized, and happier overall. We have more control over the

stress creation inside, and can we turn those patterns around and create more calm.

Our emotions exist in part to give us information. But often when we're stressed out, we are in Autopilot, too scattered among the present, past, and future to notice emotions or take them in.

Learning to hit the pause button on Motor Mind and taking Being Breaks bring us back to the present and bring more calm. These practices also allow more emotional information to surface. That's good news, and ultimately more empowering. Feeling those feelings more directly can be a huge relief.

At other times, feeling emotions more directly can be uncomfortable or even a little scary for some people.

In the next chapter, we go into how to become more comfortable with emotions in order to return to greater ease, more personal power, and Conscious Calm.

Try This:

Take a Being Break, and for five or ten minutes focus first on your breathing. Lengthening your breath, begin to put your awareness on the different sensations in your body.

Do a slow body scan: Start with bringing your attention to your feet, and move your attention up gradually from your legs, to your hips and belly, your chest and arms, all the way to your head. What sensations do you notice? Where do you feel tightness or holding? Tension, warmth or energy movement?

Focusing on one of these areas, check to see what emotion may be connected to any of these sensations. Begin to notice where in your body you feel some of the emotions underlying stress and worry. For some people this will be the stomach or chest—what about for you?

As you notice these sensations, simply breathe slowly and easily to allow the sensations to move through. Often, just putting attention on the area and lengthening your breath will help ease the more tension-filled sensations and emotions.

8

Working with Emotions

Expanding Your Comfort Zone

If you have felt stressed out and worried for a while, shifting out of Autopilot and pausing Motor Mind can bring a sense of relief. Recognizing you have a choice in what is going on internally can be a welcome surprise, and can feel freeing. Practicing Being Breaks, although new to people whose days have been filled with rushed Doing, can open the door to regaining choice and more control.

At the same time, the process of stopping Motor Mind can feel challenging. As we saw in the previous chapter, pausing both outer and inner Doing allows emotions we may not have noticed to finally get our attention.

Some of those emotions may be unfamiliar or uncomfortable. I have talked with countless people, beginning to slow down internally and take Being Breaks, who have asked me some version of, "How do I get rid of these feelings?" For some people who are starting the journey back to Being from too much Doing, feeling their emotions more directly or strongly was not part of the plan.

Yet, as we talked about in the previous two chapters, our emotions are our Internal Guidance System. They are part of a rich flow of information between brain and body, between internal and external experience, and between conscious and unconscious experience. They can provide us with information and steer us in the best direction for happiness and success. Knowing more clearly what we feel, need, and want can be a gateway to increased calm and personal power.

To know more accurately and clearly what we feel means getting better acquainted and more comfortable with emotions in the body.

Increasing Comfort with Emotions

If feeling emotions more directly seems uncomfortable to you, this simply suggests you've been in a certain comfort zone with your emotions for a while.

As you begin to take Being Breaks to stop both external and internal Doing, emotions will likely become more obvious. While that's a good thing, feeling those feelings can at first push the boundaries of an old comfort zone.

Expanding your emotional comfort zone is important for more calm and control in your life. Fortunately, because we are naturally geared toward feeling our emotions and receiving the information they provide, getting to know them is moving *with* the internal flow of the body, not against it. Your body naturally wants to give you the emotional information you most need at the moment. When we allow that information in sooner, the information doesn't have to get loud, or turn into a bodily symptom, to get our attention.

Like all learning curves, becoming more comfortable with connecting directly with emotions is a process. While it is natural to want to get over discomfort *now*, it's not accomplished by flipping a switch. It's more like growing a flower than turning on a light. As with any important learning, it takes a little practice, repetition, and patience.

Even as you begin this process, you will find that expanding your emotional comfort zone allows you to tune in to your Internal Guidance System better. Just like tuning to a radio station, a little adjustment can mean hearing the information loudly and clearly instead of garbled or through static.

It's common for certain emotions to become uncomfortable early in life. Not all families allow children to express the full range of their feelings. In some families, a child expressing emotion may be called "Too sensitive" or is given other labels. That child may learn to push feelings away.

Pushing down or avoiding those same emotions can become a habit into the teen years and adulthood. Often these are strong emotions, like anger or fear.

Some people learn to drown out emotions by becoming angry when more vulnerable feelings come up. Others try to just stay busy, to distract themselves from the emotional information percolating just under the surface, because stronger emotion in general is unfamiliar or uncomfortable.

Habitually pushing down emotions and distracting ourselves from them contributes to stress. Our emotions naturally want to give us information. We can use a lot of energy pushing important emotions away and keeping them out of our awareness.

Stress Secret #9
Pushing down emotions regularly on Autopilot
helps fuel the internal pressure cooker that helps
you stay stressed out.

We all learn to use different patterns and strategies to not feel some of our emotions as they arise. Whatever the case, part of the journey to both Conscious Calm and personal power is reclaiming our natural capacity to feel and work skillfully with our feelings.

As we feel a wider range of our emotions more directly instead of pushing them away or distracting ourselves from them, two important things begin to happen:

We have more energy for our life, because we are not using our energy to not feel certain feelings.

We have the opportunity to use the information our emotions are trying to give us. As we do so, the emotions themselves will have done their job, and often begin to fade away.

Conscious Calm Key #9
Learning to work with our emotions saves our
energy, gives us more internal and external choice
and control, and allows us to feel calm more of
the time.

An important step in expanding our emotional comfort zone is learning to view and work with our emotions as *information*.

Working with Emotions as Information

Emotions naturally show up in present time as information about our experience. Once the information has been received, emotions usually move through the body naturally and fade away.

Working with emotions more directly in this way can be new. Most of us did not get much training in how to engage with our emotions in comfortable, healthy ways as we were growing up, and it sure isn't a topic in most schools.

Many stressed-out people notice their emotions only after the feelings have become intense, when there is a sudden burst of anger or tears. Others don't notice their emotions building until they show up in the body as a stomachache, headache, or extreme tiredness.

Becoming more aware of emotions before they get so strong is part of the path to greater calm and control. It's important to remember that becoming comfortable and skilled with emotions is all learnable. With a little practice, it can become a life-changing way of Being.

Although new habits take some time, they can become second nature; it's like learning to walk or drive a car.

At first, it's so complicated and so much work. A child will lose her balance and fall over and over again before being able to get across a room in toddler steps. For a teenager or adult learning to drive a car, at first it's like juggling a hundred bits of information at once. It feels overwhelming in the beginning.

With some practice and repetition, our body memory takes over in a positive automatic way. Walking or driving a car becomes integrated, and no longer needs to be thought about, step by step. We can do the complicated balancing act of walking or the complex task of driving without thinking about how to do each part of the task.

In a similar way, engaging with emotions as information can seem complicated at first, but it does become easier with a little time.

Feeling a broader range of emotions more clearly becomes part of a new, expanded comfort zone. Having better access to our Internal Guidance System becomes an integrated, enhancing part of our life. It becomes more comfortable and second nature to us, with a little time and practice.

Emotions and Sensations in the Body

After considering that all emotions are just information, the next step is becoming more familiar with what different emotions feel like in the body.

Emotions come with physical sensation—emotions live in and are expressed through our physical body.

For many stressed-out people, the emotions can build until they start showing up as stress symptoms like headaches, sleeping difficulties, or stomach aches. Or, emotions may be felt only when they have exploded or spilled over in some way.

You may be used to feeling and recognizing a wide range of emotions, or only a few.

Either way, there is always room to expand awareness of the emotions that appear as sensation. And there is often room for learning how to feel those emotions directly, without adding any story line to them.

That common human activity is important to mention here: our tendency to add dramatic story lines to emotions, instead of feeling emotions and sensations more directly.

Emotional Information and Story Lines

Here it's time to clarify something: the information that emotions give us is NOT the same as the dramatic story we tell *about* those emotions.

For instance, let's say I have a problem at work with a demanding boss.

I am likely to have some feelings come up when my boss announces a deadline that means I'll have to work all weekend. If in my upset I tell three friends how unfair my boss is, how she is ruining my life, and how she hates me, that's all story line. I have added a narrative to what I'm feeling.

Notice that the story itself is full of strong emotions that feed and strengthen the emotions already there.

It's not that venting with our friends is bad. That's partly what friends are for—to share what's going on with us.

But if we tell only our story of upset and unfairness, those story lines can create even MORE upset.

There can seem to be a short-term payoff—we get to feel justified or righteous, and can get revenge at least behind the boss's back by telling others how wrong or evil she is.

However, when we react like this to feeling those strong feelings, we miss out on the information our emotions are giving us. That's another way we actually *participate* in keeping ourselves more stressed out and upset.

As we learned in Stress Secret #3, when we add emotional and mental energy to what Motor Mind is saying, we can add to our stress. Stress Secret #6 taught us that telling ourselves dramatic or fearful stories about past or future can keep us much more stressed, too. Telling dramatic stories about our strong feelings can do that as well. And telling stories about our feelings can also lead us to ignore or miss out on what those emotions are communicating to us.

Storytelling about our feelings can keep us from directly feeling the emotions that are stirred up, often just beneath the upset and drama. We miss out on what those emotions are trying to tell us about our experience. And we miss out on the chance to make informed choices about what we want and need in the moment.

In the job example, instead of reacting in my upset and telling people about my horrible boss, I have the option of staying with the emotions more directly.

If I choose to do that and hold off on adding a story, I am more likely to notice the tightness in my stomach and my tense breathing. I may notice some anger at the surprise new deadline, and disappointment that this deadline will mess up my weekend plans.

In staying with this more directly, I don't need to feel helpless and upset. I can remind myself that I always have choices.

I can choose to breathe more deeply, moving the tension out of my body. As that calms me, it will help me think more clearly, too. I can hold off on the story lines that are likely to make me feel tense and upset again.

If I can hold off on the story lines, I can take a look at my options and needs. Is the boss someone I can talk to, to see if the work for the deadline can be shared? If I'm stuck with it and just need to get the work done, what other kind of support do I need for the week? For the weekend? How can I strategize to make this a short-term inconvenience, instead of an ongoing crisis for me at work and in the rest of my life?

Becoming more comfortable with our emotions means staying with the emotions themselves. That means knowing what emotions are there without adding a story line to justify how we feel, defend why we feel that way, or cover up what we are feeling.

When we are better able to stay with emotions that show up, we give ourselves space to receive the information the emotions are trying to give us. We have a greater range of information about our life, and can make use of our options and choices about how to respond or act.

If we do this, we are no longer making ourselves even more stressed out. We no longer feel helpless or at the mercy of our feelings; we are less at the mercy of other people's behaviors and actions, too. And we get the chance to move toward greater calm and personal power.

While adding a story to emotion can be second nature to the mind, it's important to notice it is also a choice we make. Because we often make that choice on Autopilot, at first we may not even notice we went there. Before we know it, we're caught up in a story of how a past conversation was so terrible, or how a future interaction is going to be so stressful.

The truth is, we make a choice to add the story every time. Although this may be a strong habit, it is not a required next step after noticing an emotion—even when it's a strong feeling, like anger or fear.

We can learn to bring our attention and awareness to this version of Autopilot, too. We can hold off on story lines. Instead of making our emotions more intense and insistent with a drama, we can learn to stay with the emotions more directly. We can become more skilled at taking in the information the emotions provide, letting them come and go after they've done their job.

Staying with Emotion and Sensation

Without an exciting or intense story line pulling us back to the past or launching us into the future, it becomes easier for us to stay in present time. This naturally allows us to be more in touch with and connected to our body.

As we reconnect with ourselves in this way, we have the chance to receive more information about our experiences through our Internal Guidance System. With less stress, more information, and greater present-time bandwidth, we gain choices and options. We are then adding to our personal power instead of draining it away.

Being Breaks are an excellent way to get used to feeling emotion more directly without adding story or drama.

Once Being Breaks feel more familiar and comfortable, it can be useful to practice just noticing what emotions or sensations are in the body. Asking silently during a Being Break, "What am I feeling right now?" "What sensations are in my body?" allows you to practice simply noticing the emotions and the bodily sensations that go along with them.

To practice this, use your attention and awareness to just notice what emotions or sensations are present at the moment.

One way is to mentally name what is there with a word or two. This is called "labeling" in the practice of Mindfulness, and is used in some stress-reduction and meditation practices.[23, 24, 25]

When we simply notice and mentally label "tension in my chest" or "soft belly," we allow ourselves to be with the sensation without adding a story line to it. We can notice "discomfort in my stomach" or "a little nervousness" and just let that be, without inflating it into something more intense by adding a Motor Mind story line.

Practicing like this, we become more skilled at noticing what emotions and sensations are present. We begin to notice emotions sooner, before they have gotten super intense, or before they have turned into physical discomfort.

We also avoid creating even more stress when we hold off on telling stories about the feelings. We no longer make our emotions even more intense with drama. We feel feelings more directly. We may even notice the emotions layered underneath the first or most obvious emotion, which we would probably miss if we revved ourselves up with a dramatic story line.

In this way, we naturally expand our emotional comfort zone. We learn to just let them come up, give us information about our experience, and move on.

We become more self aware, and even more skilled in noticing that we always have internal choices and external options. We naturally become more grounded and centered, and less stressed out.

Calm becomes our central experience, instead of stress and worry.

Try This:

To practice increasing your comfort level with emotions, start with a simple Being Break. Begin by just breathing with attention for a few moments.

As you become more centered in present time and connect more with your body, allow yourself to notice what sensations are in your body as you sit just breathing. You may notice tingling, warmth, or tightness. Let yourself mentally name what you are noticing; for example, "tingling in my legs," or "a little tightness in my breath."

After a few moments of noticing and labeling the sensations, experiment with asking yourself what emotions are present in the moment. You can ask, "what am I feeling right now?" or "what emotion is here right now?"

Without getting into a story line, without making any judgments, see if you can just notice and even name what emotions are present. You might notice "nervousness" or "calm" or "sadness" or "contentment." Just allow whatever you notice to be there. As you continue breathing, see whether the sensations and emotion shift and change, just by keeping your awareness on your breath and not adding judgments or stories.

After you're done, jot down some of what you noticed or experienced.

9

Static in our Internal Guidance System

Stress and Distorted Information

When you practice working with emotions, you naturally tune in more clearly to your Internal Guidance System. You become better able to take in emotional information, and to use it skillfully to make choices that calm, empower, and free you.

As you expand your comfort zone with your emotions, you may notice that what you are feeling seems confusing, or hard to figure out. Part of that is just the process of getting used to new levels of noticing emotion. And part of it is the "static" that can exist in our Internal Guidance System, which can get in the way of hearing or feeling emotional information clearly.

Stressed-out people in particular can have a lot of static or interference in their Internal Guidance System.

Several kinds of static can make it harder to tell what we are feeling, or to receive the information from our emotions. Let's break those down.

Present-Time Static

Sometimes emotions are just strong and confusing—that alone can feel like "static" in our system.

For example, it can be difficult to tell what we're feeling when we have mixed emotions. I might really want to change something important in my life. I may even feel certain about that. But I may feel scared about the change, too. A mix of feelings—or ambivalence—can make it difficult to know what we are feeling, or to decide how to move forward.

That kind of present-time static can be reduced by bringing in more attention and awareness. Mixed feelings or ambivalence are normal, but it helps to know that's what's going on! We can then make choices using that emotional information; for example, by making a pros and cons list, or exploring what support or help we might need to feel better about taking the next step.

Then there's the kind of static in our Internal Guidance System that can happen when a lot of emotion is suddenly present. We might hear some surprising bad news (or even good news!) and feel shock, surprise, elation, sadness, confusion about what to do next, or a feeling of hesitation, and even paralysis, about what to do.

Again, this mix of strong feelings is a normal response; it's a lot of information at the same time moving through our body.

When several strong emotions come up, you can help yourself by using the tools of Conscious Calm.

You can take a Being Break to pause Motor Mind or Autopilot activity that might start up when you feel a lot all at once.

You can breathe more slowly and deeply to calm your whole system and get back to present time.

You can use grounding techniques: feeling your feet on the ground, feeling your chest and stomach move as you breathe, and connecting with your body.

All of these can help you calm your system. You will then be able to identify the different emotions more easily.

It also can help to check your internal thought vectors, and notice which directions they are pointing.

When strong feelings arise all at once, it can be easy to start thinking what I "should" do or "should" have done, or what others might think.

If you notice thought vectors pointing outward toward others who are not actually with you, and toward the past or future, you can choose to turn those arrows around. As you turn those thought arrows back toward yourself, your body, and present time, this will help calm you down. It also will help save your energy for what you actually can control in the present.

You also support yourself when you notice and name the mix of what you are feeling. Putting your attention on the emotions and naming them allows you to get back into the driver's seat of your body and mind, instead of feeling swept away by feelings that may seem out of your control.

Once you are able to notice and name even some of the emotions, you are back in a place of greater personal power and calm. It becomes easier to remember that the emotions are just information.

Static in our system can show up as stress symptoms, too.

You may notice a headache that gets stronger during the day. This can be a signal from your body. It can help to ask yourself what you need in the moment. At times of headache, tension, or pain in the body, often your body has already cranked up the volume to get your attention after failing to do so through more subtle emotions or sensations. It can be as if the body is resorting to using a loudspeaker. "Attention!! You have some feelings with some important information here!"

The headache or tension can create static in our Internal Guidance System. Emotional information may be there for us, but it can be filtered or even lost if our attention remains only on the physical discomfort.

At times like this, it's important to stop and notice that the body might be shouting at us to get our attention. Can we take a Being Break and just check in? What does the body need?

It can be something as simple as being dehydrated and needing a glass of water. Or maybe the body needs to stretch after sitting in the same position for three hours straight. Or it could be important to notice that once again we've jumped into future "what if" thinking, and we need to come back to present time. Or perhaps a current relationship is a pain in the neck!

There may be more complex information behind the headache. But if we notice only the headache and don't take it a little deeper and check our body and emotions, we can create more static and stress. By using attention and awareness, we can clear the static and get the information about what we need, what we are experiencing, or what needs to change.

Stressed-out people can have static in their Internal Guidance System because they have not yet learned to stop and notice that information is trying to get their attention.

The more you take breaks to breathe and notice what's going on in your body, and notice what choices you are making in your mind, the less stress and static in your system you will experience day to day. The more you bring in attention and awareness, the less static you'll have, and the more you will experience more calm and peace.

Past Emotion and Static

When our emotions are all about present time, it is simpler to notice internal static and take steps to calm our body and mind. When we are in a clear place, more fully in the present, we can feel emotions as they come up more easily. We can bring awareness to the information the emotions are giving us. The feelings then move on, and we can make choices according to our wants or needs, using the information we received.

However, there is another important way emotions work, and another kind of static in our Internal Guidance System.

As we've learned, emotions are supposed to come in, give us information, and move on. But when those emotions are pushed away, or seem too big or dangerous to feel, or it's not okay or safe to express them, those emotions do not have such a smooth flow.

When we push emotions out of our conscious awareness, they are often stored in the brain and body. The more intense experiences we have been through are encoded and stored not only in the brain, but in our body as well. Neuropeptides are also memory molecules, sparking our connection with or the repression of memories.[26, 27]

Anyone who has had deep massage, has experienced various energy therapies, or is a practitioner of these modalities, is likely familiar with memory coming up from the body. During a massage or energy work, memories and emotions might come up from a particular place in a person's body. A knot in the upper back, or tightness in a hip or shoulder can contain emotional information. Memories or strong emotions can come up seemingly out of nowhere when an area of the body is worked on, loosened, or opened up.

When we can't feel and express our emotions and we push them away instead, a sort of emotional reservoir forms. If we keep pushing those same feelings down, they are added to the emotional reservoir.

It takes effort and energy to keep emotions pushed down. It's a little like pushing a log under water, straight down the long way. We can push a log under the water and not see it anymore. When another log comes up, we can push that one down with our other hand. Seems like everything is fine—no logs here! But because this takes a lot of our energy, when we eventually get tired or more scattered, the logs will shoot back up.

It's the same when we push down our emotions. We may "handle" the emotions rising up by pushing them back down. And for a while it may look like we're handling everything just fine, thank you. But when we get tired, or more scattered, or more overwhelmed, those emotional logs can shoot back up. We may find ourselves suddenly angry without much reason, or in a sudden flood of tears when something small goes wrong.

This pattern is strengthened when we are mainly in Doing mode and on Autopilot.

When we are busy Doing on Autopilot, both outside in the world and inside with Motor Mind, we are not as connected to our body or to Being. When we are in that Autopilot Doing state, when our emotions show up to give us information, we may not notice fully, or we may push them aside and keep Doing. We may try to distract ourselves, or numb the emotions with food or other substances.

The emotions may seem to go away, but they do not. Because they have information for our well being, emotions naturally persist. They might become stronger, even after we have pushed them down beneath our conscious awareness. It's like pushing those logs temporarily under water; we may tell ourselves we don't see them anymore, so they must be gone. But they haven't really gone anywhere.

Just as with holding logs under water, it takes energy to hold emotions out of our conscious awareness when they are trying to get our attention. A kind of static is created in our Internal Guidance System when we use our energy to push or numb the feelings out of our awareness. We are essentially saying "no, I don't want to know" as the emotions arise.

Many people dive even more into Doing to keep feelings at bay. This can create a cycle of not hearing the emotional information through the static, and generating even more static by pushing down or numbing the feelings out. This creates even more energy drain and stress, because of the distraction and the hard work of keeping the emotions out of awareness.

The emotions we push down most frequently also have emotional information for us. However, that information is usually about the *past*, not the present.

There is an easy way to tell if an emotion is giving us information from past experiences rather than a present experience. Emotions are energy (e-motion is sometimes broken down as energy-motion). Our emotions can be thought of as energy moving through our body with information. When an emotion is part of the old emotions reservoir, outside of our conscious awareness, it has a certain energy, frequency, or feel to it. When something happens in present time that has a similar feel or emotional frequency to it, we can react with feelings not only from the present, but also from the past reservoir that spills over into present time. Our reaction will be stronger than necessary, fueled by past feelings.

Triggers and Button Pushing

The dynamic of past feelings spilling over into the present is often called being "triggered."

When there is a trigger in present time, it reminds us of past experiences and emotions, and brings up old, unexpressed emotions from the past. With all of that emotion from both present and past, our reaction can be out of proportion to what just happened in the moment.

This dynamic is also referred to as "having your buttons pushed." The behavior or words we react to in the moment have an emotional effect in present time, of course. But when we are triggered, those words or the behavior also push old buttons, touching off the reservoir of old emotion, which spills into present time.

This naturally can create confusion and problems in more than one way.

When our reaction is too big for what just happened, people around us can feel confused. They might become emotionally shut down, or become more reactive themselves. Responses like "What's the big deal?" "Why are you going off?" "What just happened?" can be hints that past emotions were triggered and are spilling into the present in confusing ways.

For example, Jay had a dad who often criticized him in anger when he was growing up. Jay learned quickly as a child that he couldn't get angry at his father for this unfair treatment; it only made his dad's anger more intense. So Jay naturally felt anger arise (anger can tell us when our boundaries are being violated or when there is an injustice; this is some of the information anger can give us). However, Jay had needed to learn to push anger down quickly and not express it, because expressing his anger would not have been safe.

Without even realizing it, Jay learned to push anger away and hold anger and other strong feelings in. This became a habit for Jay, and a natural way of being for him as he grew older that just felt normal. He ended up appearing to be a quiet kind of guy, maybe a little subdued or shy.

When Jay got involved in his first serious relationship, a pattern began to emerge. Often, when his girlfriend Allie reminded him he hadn't yet done something, or when she gave him a suggestion, the usually quiet Jay would explode. He would accuse Allie of being overly critical, and his anger would confuse and sometimes scare her.

Jay was being triggered by what he heard as his girlfriend's criticism. For him, even a reminder he hadn't done something could trigger the energy of his father's criticism and his own, unexpressed anger from back then. Now as a grown-up, anger often would come rushing up when "criticism" seemed to be in the air, especially from someone Jay cared about.

Two important things were happening in this scenario. First, the old static in Jay's internal guidance system prevented him from hearing that his girlfriend was not being mean or overly critical like his dad had been. He was hearing what she said through a filter from the past. This kind of static creates a filter from the past over present time, and distorts present-time communication. Hearing things in a distorted way prevented Jay from accurately hearing and responding to his girlfriend's communication.

Jay's being triggered by this "criticism" also brought the reservoir of old anger into the present. That old anger did hold information about Jay's anger at his father, but that was information about the *past*.

Old, pushed-down emotions from our reservoir cannot give us accurate information about the present. Jay ended up distorting what he heard from his girlfriend, and reacting much more strongly than appropriate in the moment.

Once Jay learned how to notice his triggers, and learned about his reservoir of old anger and how to heal it, he became more in control. He was able to hear the information his reservoir of old anger held about his childhood experiences, in the correct context, where it belonged. He also was better able to stay calm in the moment, and hear Allie in present time. He became better at responding to what she was actually saying to him, instead of exploding with old anger that did not belong in his present-time relationship.

Our reservoirs of old emotion create a powerful kind of static.

We have some of this going on all the time. Our mind refers to the past (out of habit) to respond to the present. This occurs in some necessary ways (like knowing we call that thing over there a "chair"). It also happens in other more distorted, unnecessary ways, which is one reason we misinterpret or miscommunicate with others.

Some of that is minor confusion that can be easily straightened out. Other times, as in Jay's case, it causes more serious problems in the present because the static and the emotional reactions are so strong.

It is important to recognize when a reservoir of old emotion frequently comes up, distorting our present interactions and affecting us and those around us.

One way is to notice when we react more strongly than the current situation calls for. A present situation may be a little sad, but if we cry for a long time or get despondent, old emotions are also being triggered.

Or, in another situation, frustration may be an understandable response. But if we instead get furious, we are being triggered, and the old reservoir of emotion is spilling over into the present in ways that are out of proportion.

That older reservoir of emotion DOES have important information for us, as emotions often do. However, a triggered emotional reservoir brings emotional information about the *past*, not the present.

When we are triggered, if we assume that all of the feelings, all of the emotional information, is about the present and we act on it, we will distort what is happening in present time. We also might say something or behave in ways that hurt others or confuse them. We might make a situation worse and even more stressful, instead of clearing it up through more skillful present-time communication.

When we are triggered by emotions from the past, we are experiencing present time partly through the emotions of the past. If we assume all of the emotions are about now, our hearing can be distorted by that static.

Here is a more visual image: when we are triggered, it is as if we are looking at the present through a filter of the past that has come up in front of our eyes.

Either way we think about it, when we are in a triggered, reactive state, if we assume all of our feelings are about the present, we cannot perceive the present accurately. We are quite likely to overreact, miscommunicate, or judge inaccurately or unfairly.

In Jay's case, his triggered anger was more intense than the situation called for, and his girlfriend felt hurt, scared, and confused. Allie finally threatened to leave him if he didn't get a handle on his anger. As Jay learned about the reservoir of anger and his triggers, he was better able to separate out past information from present time. He learned to practice breathing through some of his feelings, in order to stay calmer and in the present. Jay then was able to keep his relationship with Allie, and their communication became better than before.

Working with Static from the Past

In Jay's case, when Allie gave him an ultimatum about their relationship, he chose to get counseling. With the help of a counselor who understood the effects of past emotions on the present, Jay was able to learn to separate out his past emotions from the present. He learned to take in the information from the past, which the reservoir was presenting, and do some healing from his complex childhood.

That is one way to "drain" a reservoir of old emotions: learn to take the information those old emotions are providing, and use them to heal old wounds and be happier, calmer, and more in control. For some people it can be helpful to consult with someone who has experience and training in this kind of emotional healing.

Consulting with a professional can be especially important when reservoirs of old emotions are from complex childhood experiences, or from the trauma of physical, emotional, or sexual abuse. In those cases trying to sort out what is going on can be difficult without the help of an experienced professional. For many people it can be important to get a consultant and helper in the path to healing. In doing so, it is vital to find someone experienced in trauma and healing, and with whom you feel comfortable. (See the Resources section for more information.)

For others, it can be enough to bring more awareness to the times that a reservoir of old emotions is being triggered. With increased awareness, as usual, there is more choice. Many techniques can be used to help safely move old emotion when it gives us information about the past. Journaling, music, exercise, slower movement like yoga or Tai Chi, art, and other creative activities can all be useful. Participating in these activities can help take in emotional information, and move emotions through and out of the body.

Using Being Breaks and breathing can also be key in creating more internal space and calm in situations or contexts in which we are reactive or triggered. Breath and Being are especially useful in bringing greater calm to times of triggering and feeling unexpressed emotion. Since Being Breaks help train us to stay more in present time, we are less in Autopilot, and less at the apparent mercy of Motor Mind. We are able to see more clearly what is going on in our mind and body, and receive the information our body is trying to give us. We become better able to sort out whether an emotion is connected to a reservoir of the past, and make choices that calm and empower us.

Try This:

Notice the next time you have a reaction to something or someone that seems stronger than may be called for. This may show up as a strong wave of emotion, or you may catch Motor Mind telling upset or intense stories.

When you notice this, take a few breaths to bring yourself back to your body and present time. Then see if you can name some of the triggered emotions. Are they familiar? Is this a frequent trigger pattern, or is it more rare? What is some of the information about the past that these emotions might be holding?

10

Clearing the Static, Part I

Finding Calm in the Storm

Experiencing static in the Internal Guidance System can be like stormy emotional weather. Noticing when different kinds of static have shown up in your system gives you the choice and chance to clear the static and return to greater calm. Having various tools in your Inner Tool Kit can help clear the static and strengthen Conscious Calm.

Some of the tools we have already discussed can be useful in clearing emotional static. They can help when it's hard to tell what you are feeling, or when many emotions are swirling at once.

When the static has to do with external and internal Autopilot Doing (that would be "Do-It-Yourself Static"), Being Breaks can help clear the static quickly. The key is to dial up awareness when you know your body and mind are in some tension or turbulence, when it's hard to tell exactly what you are feeling.

Present-time, Do-It-Yourself static and stress can be easier to undo.

As we have discussed, when you dial up your awareness and attention, you are interrupting the patterns of Autopilot and Motor Mind. When you choose to take a Being Break, those patterns can be weakened further. If you choose to stop outer and inner Doing and bring yourself back to Being, you will be able to identify your body's emotions or sensations more easily. Based on what you notice, you then can make additional choices, based on what you want or need next.

Breath is another familiar tool that can help clear the static of confusing emotion.

When you have used your awareness to notice that Autopilot has crept back in, or when external Doing has become more pressured, it's time for a break. Your choice to pause already helps clear the static. It's a way of taking back your personal power—you are back in charge again, making a proactive choice, instead of feeling at the mercy of your emotions or thoughts.

Then, when you choose to take ten slower, deep breaths, our friend the vagus nerve is activated. Those deeper, slower breaths will allow your entire system to begin calming down.

As you take your outside and inside speed down a notch, you return to Being from the external and internal Doing. You then will be able to feel what is happening in your body more clearly. It will be easier to identify sensations and emotions. The confusing static will lessen, and may even disappear entirely. You will be left with greater clarity and calm.

Maintaining a connection with your breath throughout the day can help minimize static in the system. It can help you catch Autopilot and Motor Mind as they rev up, and help you return to Being. Breathing with awareness during the day can reconnect you with your body, with Being, and with present time, when static has gotten in the way of your clarity and calm.

Stopping the Story Line

As we have discussed, creating inner stories is a dynamic we create by choice, but often while we are in Autopilot. When we humans feel a strong emotion, we often automatically add a story line about it. This often adds more stress to our system as our thoughts and feelings build and intensify, based on the story we tell.

So another way to stop creating more static, tension, and stress in our system is to bring our awareness to this habit. If we stop ourselves from starting a story, we instantly have more choice. We can choose to put our awareness directly on the emotion that comes up, *without* adding a story line.

This can be tricky, especially at first. Many of us are used to knowing our emotions and life through the stories of "What just happened to me" or "What she said" or "What he did" or "I'm so pissed off right now because…"

It's a big step toward both personal power and calm when we learn to pull back on the thought vectors that we create *about* our emotions. We may be in the habit of shooting those energized thought arrows back into the past ("What he/she did to me" "What I should have done or said") or into the future ("What if I can't do it?" "What if I say something wrong and they think I'm stupid?").

Instead of launching the familiar thought arrows into the past or the future, we can learn to stop before we've gone too far with a story.

With practice, we can keep our awareness more on the body and the feelings there. When we keep our awareness in the present and don't engage in a story line, we have more information about what is happening now, both internally and externally. We then have more choice, too. We are out of Autopilot, and back in the realms of personal power, choice, and Conscious Calm.

Surprisingly, when we notice emotions arising and do not add a story to them, the feelings often move through faster.

But this also is not so surprising. When we simply put our awareness on emotions and notice what they are, we no longer add fuel to the emotional fire with our story. We also allow ourselves to feel our body's sensations—tension, warmth, or energy movement. We can take in the information emotions have for us, and allow them to move on. We are allowing our Internal Guidance System to do its job, without any added static or interference from our elaborate stories of unfairness or fear or insecurity.

Breath is another huge help in feeling emotion or sensation without adding a story line to it. If you practice using your breath while feeling emotion or sensation, you will naturally notice that Autopilot Motor Mind may start up a story or commentary. It's an old and deep mental habit for all of us humans.

When you notice Motor Mind revving up (or maybe after it already has!), bring your awareness back to your body and your breathing. Take a few deeper breaths to help quiet the mind and move the emotion through. This will help you anchor to present time, and the pull to create a story about the emotion will lessen. You will reduce stress and tension instead of creating more. You will be using your personal power, making a conscious choice to return to calm, instead of letting old mental habits and emotions run you.

Big Benefits

This practice of feeling emotion directly without starting a story about the feelings is not easy, but it is hugely helpful in several ways.

First, feeling emotion without a story keeps you from adding more fuel to the emotional fire and creating even more static in your Internal Guidance System.

Second, without a story line grabbing your attention, you can connect with your breath as you feel what's happening in your body. This allows the vagus nerve system to calm your body.

Third, when you feel emotions more directly, you are helping yourself tune in to the information the emotions are trying to give you. You are giving yourself the chance to make better choices based on what you need or want in the moment, instead of reacting to emotions that may come from your story line.

Finally, you allow emotions to do their job of providing information about your experience, and move on. Without a story, your emotions can come and go as they are meant to do, instead of continuing to swirl or being pushed down into an emotions reservoir, only to come back up later.

Boundaries and Static

Entire books have been written about good boundaries. Here we will talk about a few of the ways you can use boundaries to clear emotional static and stress when you notice it, and prevent static and stress from building up in your life.

What is a good boundary, anyway?

A good boundary can mean having clarity about where one person's feelings or personal business begins and ends. Of course, the definition of a "good" boundary can differ hugely across families, cultures, and societies. It's a complex term with many variations, depending on the context. I'll try to keep it simple.

With boundaries in a relationship, when emotional static is present, it can help to consider whether you are taking responsibility for someone else's emotions or actions. In general, it's wise to take responsibility only for those things you can control, and for what is actually yours. Taking responsibility for something you cannot control can lead to emotional and mental static, and is a pretty good recipe for both stress and worry.

Creating a clearer boundary within yourself can help with this. For example, you may notice Motor Mind activity or excessive worry about someone else, especially if you can't control what you are most worried about.

You can double-check: whose is this? Is it really mine, or is it the other person's? A Being Break or connecting with breath can help you come back to yourself in the present, to what is yours and to what you can control. It's a way of creating an internal boundary; instead of mushing up what's yours and someone else's, and mixing up future and present time, you can land more clearly back in the present and in the territory of what is actually yours.

Creating good boundaries with time can help clear static, and can help prevent stress from building up in the first place.

For example, I've lost count of the number of people who have told me that they return from a day at work and just can't leave the work behind. Whether it's a looming deadline, a challenging co-worker, or workplace gossip, many people come home physically, but their mind is still at work.

Doing this creates a disconnect from present time and from your body. It creates static and more stress, because you're disconnected from present time, and therefore from your body and its signals.

In addition, it leads you to miss out on being at home. Friends and loved ones may notice you're not fully there. Or you may end up feeling like you just want to sit in front of the television or at the computer to drown out Motor Mind for a while. That might feel okay in the short run, but it's actually creating even more static in your system, and pushing away the sensations and emotions that may be trying to get your attention.

Instead, it can help if you consciously choose to create stronger time boundaries.

As an example, as you start the day at your workplace, breathe and ground yourself in your body and in the present. Be as fully at work as you can be; deliberately leave what's going on at home, at home.

Similarly, when you come home, be aware of the fact that you are no longer at work! Bring your full self, not just your body, back home.

Use Being Breaks or some of the suggestions below to create a better boundary between work time and at-home time. You'll have less static and more fun. You'll be less stressed, and better able to enjoy yourself and your life.

Shifting Gears

Our focus with Conscious Calm is mainly on the internal choices that can reduce stress and promote calm. But when it comes to clearing emotional static, some external activities can be a big help.

Use some of the examples below when you want to clear the static of too much mental Doing, or when emotions are strong and confusing. These activities can help you shift gears from Doing back to Being when Motor Mind gets going, or when you are transitioning back home after work. Some of these activities also can help you move your emotions through your body, reducing emotional static and stress.

Physical Activity

Physical activity like walking, jogging, or other exercise is excellent for shifting internal gears. Physical exercise has all of the benefits you probably already know about, including adding oxygen throughout the system and shifting the body's bio-chemistry in ways that reduce stress. Moving your body with exercise or dance also helps move emotion through.

Many people find they are in a noticeably different, better emotional and mental state after going for a walk, dancing for a while, or going for a bike ride. Even fifteen or twenty minutes of one of these activities can clear your head and clear emotional static from your system.

Slower forms of physical activity can be excellent for shifting internal gears, as well.

Examples include gentler forms of yoga, Tai Chi, Chi Gong, and many martial arts. These all include instructions that promote and support awareness and Being. They are a natural fit for anyone who wants to add more Being into a busy life. And these slower physical activities are deceptive—they are a good workout, too. They may look slower and less intense than running, for example. But these slower systems of movement exercise both the physical muscles and joints of the body and the energy circulatory system, for a full internal workout.

Creative Arts

The creative arts, including art, music, and crafts, are all things to Do, but also provide the chance to shift into Being.

You may already know the feeling of getting lost in an activity and not realizing how much time has gone by. Many people experience a sense of "flow" when they immerse themselves in an activity they love.[28] This, too, can promote Being and living in present time. Allowing yourself space for creative activities you enjoy is another way to allow internal static to clear.

Time in Nature

Nature may be the ultimate model of Being. That's why spending time outside in Nature can help shift us from Doing and Motor Mind mode back into Being.

Head out into Nature when it's possible for you. If you don't have that opportunity, spend some time in a garden at home, or even with house plants. These, too, can be a way to shift gears back into present time and Being, and another way to clear static.

Of course if you have a pet or pets, you already know that they are masters of Being. Choosing to spend a little time with a beloved pet can be a good way to shift internal modes and clear static, as well.

Community

We are by nature social beings. We need to spend time with people we feel connected to.

For some people this may be biological family. For others, it may be chosen family, or a close group of friends. For still others, it's a community built around a common activity, a common social or political goal, or shared values. It can be a religious institution, or a spiritual group of like-minded people.

Whatever your chosen community connections, remind yourself to reconnect with those people or groups, especially when things have felt stressful, or when you have felt a lot of internal static. Check to see whether you want to be in a bigger community group, or just need one-on-one time with a good friend. Reconnecting with others can be a helpful way to shift internal gears, clear internal static, and help us feel more connected and calmer.

Getting clearer mentally and emotionally is a basic part of the Conscious Calm path. Clearing our emotional static is a key part of this. In the next chapter, we'll explore a power tool for clearing static.

Try This:

Jot down your responses to these three questions:

When do you tend to add an internal story to emotion? Is it usually about a particular event? A specific person?

See if you can notice when those internal stories get going. Pick one situation and try stopping the story to just notice the emotion.

What activities do you already enjoy that could serve as a way to shift gears when you experience static in your Internal Guidance System?

How might you include time in your week for one or more of those activities?

11

Clearing the Static, Part II

A Stress-Busting Power Tool

In addition to your Conscious Calm tools of breath, Being Breaks, and noticing emotion without a story line, there is another technique that is simply one of best stress-busting tools around.

This stress-management technique is easy to learn. Like the breath, it is another tool you can always have with you.

You may already have heard about EFT, or Tapping. Emotional Freedom Techniques was developed by Gary Craig in the 1990s (see the Resources section for more information about EFT).

Tapping uses the body's energy circulation system, or meridian system. If you are familiar with acupuncture or acupressure, these modalities also use the body's network of energy circulation pathways to help energy circulation improve, strengthening organs and systems of the body.

EFT is one of many Energy Psychology techniques that use the body's energy system to help shift or clear emotions. While some of these techniques have caused controversy in the world of standard psychotherapy, for trained and experienced practitioners of many of these modalities (EFT and other Energy Psychology techniques), they are a revolution in emotional healing. [29, 30]

EFT is often called "acupuncture for feelings without the needles" because it uses the body's meridian system to address the energetic disruption or emotional static discussed in previous chapters.[31] By tapping on specific points—mainly on the head and upper body—while holding a problem or source of static in mind, EFT helps clear static and lower emotional intensity.[32, 33, 34]

Because EFT is practical, easy to learn and use on your own, and is often effective quickly, it can be a power tool for stress relief.

Because tapping is done on your physical body, it helps to bring you out of Motor Mind activity and back to the body and present time. Since you focus first on the source of your static or current emotional intensity, this also helps bring you back to the present, and to your current physical sensations and emotions. Then the tapping sequence helps ease the emotional static.

There is also a nice side effect I've noticed since I began using EFT in my work with clients in 1999, and other practitioners report the same thing. After a round or two of tapping, people usually feel more relaxed, no matter what the initial issue or problem. For many people, EFT becomes a favorite tool for returning to calm and greater relaxation when outside events are stressful, or when internal Autopilot and static patterns sneak back in.

EFT Basics

Below is a description of how to do basic EFT or Tapping, and some examples of how to use it to relieve stress and worry in the moment. You also can see the Resources section for information about using

EFT in more complex ways, including to help with more layered emotional patterns and trauma.

Here, as usual, we will keep it simple.

As a practice example, let's assume you are feeling stressed and worried. You remember to take a Being Break and use deeper breaths, and then you notice tension in your chest and some nervousness.

When using EFT, we rate the intensity of what you are feeling from zero (meaning no intensity at all) to ten (meaning it couldn't be any more intense). So in our example, let's say that the tension in the chest is at five, and the nervousness feels like about a four. (You may want to check and see if there is any tension in your chest right now, and if so, give that tension a number from zero to ten as you practice.)

This is then our starting point for EFT. We tap on one aspect of an issue at a time, because being specific helps the tapping to be more effective. We start by tapping on the aspect with the highest intensity, in order to feel better faster. In our practice example, that would be "tension in my chest" at an intensity level of five. (Use your actual intensity number here.)

Whenever we begin a round of EFT, we start with what is called the "EFT Set-up." The Set-Up helps with any mixed feelings that may exist about the issue we are tapping on.

We often have mixed feelings when we want to change something about ourselves. We may want to lose an extra few pounds, but we also want that dessert. We may want less tension in our body, but we also may be so angry at someone that it's hard to let the anger go. That kind of ambivalence is natural, and is very common with change.

Because ambivalence or mixed emotions can also show up in our energy system, EFT addresses this right away. The Set-Up helps clear ambivalence in the system, and allows the tapping to work more effectively. So whenever we begin a round of EFT, we always start by doing the Set-Up first.

EFT Set-Up

Begin by tapping on what's called the Karate-Chop point. This point is on the fleshy side of the hand (where you would karate chop something if you were so inclined). Tap repeatedly on this point. Using two fingers is fine, and using either hand is okay. The tapping should be firm enough to stimulate the meridian point, but not so hard that it hurts!

While tapping continuously on the Karate-Chop point, say the Set-Up Phrase three times out loud, a little louder than your usual speaking voice:

"Even though I feel this tension in my chest, I want to deeply and completely love and accept myself anyway."

It's not important to believe these statements; they are not affirmations. The EFT Set-Up simply helps you name both sides of any ambivalence that might be in your system and clear the ambivalence. It's letting your body and mind know that even though you have this problem, you're okay.

After repeating the Set-Up Phrase three times while tapping on the Karate-Chop point, move into the first section of tapping.

EFT Tapping Points

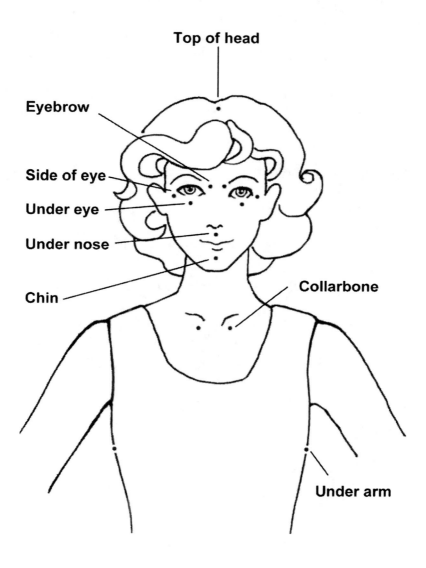

EFT Tapping Section – Part 1

After the Set-Up, you will tap on different points, mainly on the head and upper body (see Figure 1).

As you tap, always use a "Reminder Phrase" with each point to help keep the focus on the issue you are addressing. With the practice example, you would use "This tension in my chest" as you tap on each point five or six times (or so—this does not need to be exact).

So using the example, you tap on each point and repeat "This tension in my chest" with each one. Below are the points with the Reminder Phrase:

Eyebrow (EB): "This tension in my chest"

Outside of the eye (OE): "This tension in my chest"

Under the eye (UE): "This tension in my chest"

Under the nose (UN): "This tension in my chest"

Chin point (CP): "This tension in my chest"

Collar bone points (CB): "This tension in my chest"

Under the arm (UA): "This tension in my chest"

Brain Balancing Section

After the initial tapping, you will do the middle section of the EFT protocol.

This is called the Brain Balancing section, because you activate one brain hemisphere and then the other by humming, counting, and eye movements. (This can feel a little weird at first, but just go with it and see what you experience.)

Do all of this while tapping on what's called the Gamut Spot on the back of the hand, between the ring-finger and pinkie-finger knuckles.

For the Brain Balancing section, tap continuously on the Gamut Spot and hold your head straight. While you continue the tapping, do the following nine things:

Close your eyes

Open your eyes

Keeping your head straight, look hard down and to the right

Look hard down and to the left

Just with your eyes, make a slow, big, wide circle in one direction

Change directions and make another slow, wide circle with your eyes, not moving your head

As you keep tapping, hum a random tune for a few seconds

Count to five out loud: "1, 2, 3, 4, 5"

Hum a random tune again for a few seconds

That's the Brain Balancing section. It is also called the Nine Gamut, because you are doing nine different things while tapping on the Gamut Spot.

EFT Tapping Section – Part 2

After the Brain Balancing section, you will return to tapping on the points you started with, again repeating the reminder phrase "This tension in my chest" with each tapping point:

Eyebrow Point (EB) "This tension in my chest"

Outside of the eye (OE): "This tension in my chest"

Under the eye (UE): "This tension in my chest"

Under the nose (UN): "This tension in my chest"

Chin point (CP): "This tension in my chest"

Collar Bone points (CB): "This tension in my chest"

Under the arm (UA): "This tension in my chest"

And finally, because the meridian pathways all end at the top of the head, I always suggest that you end by tapping on the crown of the head. Use either the flat of your hand or your fingers bunched up. So the last tapping point of the full EFT round is:

Crown of head (CH): "This tension in my chest"

That completes one full round of EFT.

After finishing the full protocol, take a deep breath and let it out completely. Keep your attention on your body, and notice what you notice. You may feel warmth or tingling in your hands or fingers. You may be aware of some energy movement in your legs or feet. You might feel a little more relaxed in general. Just notice what's there for a few moments.

Then check in again with the level of tension in your chest. Bring your attention to the chest area and recall your intensity number. See if that number has gone up, gone down, or stayed the same.

In most cases the intensity level will have dropped a point or more.

Occasionally the intensity level goes UP at first. When that occurs, usually one of three things is happening:

Focusing on the problem or sensation led you to feel the emotions more directly

Saying the issue out loud brought up a little more feeling

Some emotions underlying the problem came forward more clearly

If you experience a rise in intensity after the first practice round, know that this initial rise in intensity sometimes happens, and that it is likely due to one of the reasons above. An additional round or two usually helps bring the intensity level back down.

Additional Rounds of EFT

The protocol for EFT after the first round changes only a little. The structure and tapping points all stay the same; there are just small adjustments to the language of the Set-Up and Reminder Phrases.

Using our example, let's say the intensity level of "tension in my chest" went from five to three after the first round. This would be a typical change after doing one full EFT tapping sequence.

For the second round (and all following rounds), do the Set-Up by tapping on the Karate-Chop point again, and repeat three times a slight variation of the Set-Up Phrase:

"Even though I *still* have *some remaining* tension in my chest, I want to deeply and completely love and accept myself anyway."

Using the words "still have some remaining" tension allows us and our whole system to hear the message that the tension is getting lower and is on its way out.

The tapping points stay the same during the additional rounds of EFT. The Reminder Phrase changes slightly to match the Set-Up Phrase. Tapping each point, repeat "This *remaining* tension in my chest." This reminder phrase also helps the entire system hear that the tension and emotional static are on their way out of the body.

Always end every round of EFT by taking a deep breath and noticing what you can notice in the body. After that, check back in with the remaining tension in your chest (or whatever the sensation is) and give the remaining intensity a number from zero to ten.

Usually the intensity numbers will drop some with each round of EFT. It's important to bring the intensity level down to zero whenever possible.

This is good practice, especially for stressed-out people. I often have people tell me, "Oh, it's down to a three; I feel better, that's fine." For people who have been walking around with tension or other intensity levels of seven or eight, having the intensity drop to a three can feel much better. That's good, but we want to practice *completely* clearing the emotional static or unneeded emotional intensity. The goal within reach is emotional freedom. There's no need to walk around with a smaller burden of intensity, saying that it's so much better than the bigger load before, when you can put the entire burden down

Using EFT When Feeling "Stressed Out"

Because the phrase "stressed out" is often shorthand for all kinds of emotions, it's good to name more exactly what emotions and sensations are present.

We already covered the value of naming emotions and sensations in Chapters 8 and 9. When using EFT, identifying specific emotions and sensations is also important, because the more specific the Set-Up Phrase and the Reminder Phrase are, the more effective EFT tends to be.

For example, if you try to tap on "Even though I'm so stressed out…" as the Set-Up Phrase, and you tap using "so stressed out" on each of the tapping points, you are likely to feel some relief. However, if you take a moment to check to see what emotions and sensations are present, and use those more precise emotions in the tapping, you can accomplish faster relief through more effective tapping.

This is because "stressed out" is the umbrella category for many emotions and sensations. Each of those emotions and sensations is a separate, more specific aspect of feeling "stressed out."

When referring to EFT, we often talk about comparing an issue or problem to a small forest of trees. If we tap on the whole "forest," there may be some relief, but it is likely to take longer.

However, if we identify the highest intensity "trees" in that forest and tap each one down, two things tend to occur. One, faster relief is achieved on each of the aspects. And two, because EFT tends to have a generalizing effect, we do not have to tap on each individual "tree" in the entire "forest" for the static to clear. We may need to tap on several of the related "trees" or aspects of a general issue, and the rest of the "trees" usually fall and lose their intensity as well. Then the entire "forest" or general issue loses the emotional intensity that it contained before the tapping.

So, tapping on "stressed out" can be useful. But EFT usually will be more effective if you break down feeling "stressed out" into the specific emotions and the physical sensations you are feeling.

For example, let's say you discover three major aspects of feeling "stressed out": tension in your shoulders at a three, nervousness at a five, and tight breathing at a seven. You would start with "tightness in my breathing"—the aspect with the highest intensity—and create a specific Set-Up Phrase:

"Even though I feel this tightness in my breathing, I deeply and completely love and accept myself anyway."

The Reminder Phrase with each tapping point would then be "this tightness in my breathing," or "this tightness in my breath," or "this tightness in my chest"—whichever feels more correct or resonant to you at the time.

Once the intensity of "tightness in my breath" has come down to a zero or close to it, you then check the level of the other two aspects, "nervousness" and "tension in my shoulders." Often, although you are tapping specifically on something else, the other intensity levels also go down.

You then would pick the highest remaining intensity level to work on next. Perhaps that is "tension in my shoulders." You would create a specific Set-Up Phrase and Reminder according to the pattern above, and tap this and other remaining aspects as close to zero as you can.

Working with more specific emotion or sensation is the most efficient way to use EFT to reduce the various kinds of emotional and physical intensity that can be a part of feeling "stressed out."

Tips for Using EFT Effectively

As you practice EFT, keep these points in mind for the best results:

Practice the complete EFT protocol while you're learning. While many people teach shortcut versions, in my experience doing the full round, including the Brain Balancing section, often gives people better and faster results.

At the same time, if you forget one of the points, don't worry about it. The EFT protocol is the same for all issues because more than enough meridian points are used for each issue or problem.

Make the Set-Up Phrase as specific as possible. Remember that if the intensity you are feeling is something more general like "stressed out" or "worried," it's best to check in first with what specific emotions or sensations are present in the body, and tap on those individually.

Use sensations in the body whenever possible, not concepts. For instance, tapping on "feeling like a loser" is not likely to be very effective because "loser" is a judgment and a concept. But if something happened and you judge yourself as a "loser," check the emotions underneath. You might find embarrassment, shame, or even the dynamic of "being critical of myself." You could tap on these one at a time. Another effective way would be to identify what you feel in your body when you feel embarrassed or are being critical of yourself, and tap on each of those sensations.

If there is sudden, strong emotion or you are feeling overwhelmed, just start tapping to reduce the intensity without sorting it out first. Always start with whatever is most intense, like "Even though I'm feeling all this overwhelm..." When the intensity level goes down and you feel some relief, then check to see what other aspects, emotions, or sensations are present, and tap on those one at a time.

Be persistent. While there are many instances of EFT clearing an aspect or a simple issue in just a few rounds, some problems or emotional intensity can take more tapping in order for you to feel relief.

Use language that sounds most true for you. For example, "this headache" may be accurate, but "this throbbing in my temples" may resonate more. When the language of the Set-Up and Reminder Phrases is more resonant and specific, the tapping is often more effective.

It's important to know that using EFT can be like peeling an onion layer by layer. As you tap one layer of emotional intensity away, another layer of emotion can come up from either the present or the past, bringing up emotional information.

Once the intensity level is cleared from one layer or aspect (or "tree in the forest"), you will often be able to feel the next-highest "tree" more clearly. At times that can be a surprise. When these emotions are part of the emotional reservoir from the past, your tapping work can be more complex. It can be challenging to track what is from present time, and what is emotional information from the past.

Some people do this more layered work on their own with success. Others prefer to have an experienced practitioner's help. It's important to consider getting guidance and support when old emotions involve trauma or complex emotions and memories from childhood. In that case it's best to work with a licensed professional who is experienced in trauma and works with EFT. (See the Resources section.)

As a stress-busting power tool, EFT can be very useful to work with on your own with current static in the emotional system.

Try tapping when it's hard to stop Motor Mind and you feel tension in your body from revved-up thinking and feeling. Or try EFT when you catch yourself thinking you are feeling "stressed" or "stressed out." Notice the sensations or feelings in your body as specifically as you can. Give the sensations a number from zero to ten so you can track your progress. Find the aspect with the highest intensity level, and start the tapping sequence from there.

Using EFT like this can be one of the quickest ways to clear emotional static and stress from your system. It can be a power tool for your tool kit when you want to bring yourself out of a pattern of stress and worry and back to greater relaxation and calm.

Try This:

Try using EFT as a Stress-Busting tool at a specific time during the day.

Some people choose to stop in the middle of the day and do a round or two. Others use EFT when they finish work, as a way to clear any leftover static. Pick a time that works for you.

Choose a sensation you notice in your body—it could be tension somewhere, or "thinking too much," or "this work headache." Note the intensity level when you start, keep the tapping simple, and do two or three rounds. See where the intensity level is after finishing those rounds. Notice how your body feels overall.

Try doing a round or two of tapping at that time for a week. Notice how you feel after doing this for seven days in a row.

12

Walking the Path

Daily Steps to Nourish Calm

Being able to clear the static in your Internal Guidance System gives you greater control over stress and worry. Taking Being Breaks, engaging your breath, changing the direction of your thought vectors, and EFT can help break up old internal patterns, and create an opening for you to experience greater calm and peace in your life.

There is one more idea I want to introduce you to. It's another huge benefit to clearing static and moving toward Conscious Calm. It helps explain how your path of Conscious Calm is also the path to enhancing your personal power and effectiveness. My hope is that it will motivate you even more to add some of these Conscious Calm practices into your life and transform stress into well being.

Coherence

When we experience static in our emotions, our thoughts and feelings can feel like they are all over the place. This is also true on an energetic level. As we discussed in Chapter 6, when our thought vectors are directed mainly outside of ourselves and to past and future, our attention and energy are divided and scattered. This is a kind of energetic disorder that can be measured on both biological and energetic levels.

The opposite of this energetically messy state is called "coherence."

Coherence is order in a system. In a basic sense, it's when energies line up or are in synch instead of going in random directions.

Coherence is used to describe this "lining up" in both physics and biology. One scientist who has described coherence is Dr. William Tiller, a professor emeritus who worked at Stanford's Department of Materials Science for over thirty years.

Dr. Tiller gives many examples of coherence in physics and in our body.[35] He describes the power of coherence with the example of a basic light bulb.

The light waves in a light bulb are normally shooting off in many directions. They are incoherent. They do give off light; it's just that the light waves are not all going in the same direction at once.

Dr. Tiller gives an example of what could happen if a regular light bulb's light waves became completely orderly. There are inaccurate quotes about this floating around the Internet, but Dr. Tiller kindly provided the correct quote. Dr. Tiller explains that if we shifted a regular 60-watt light bulb…

"… from its normally incoherent state to the coherent state, then, the energy intensity at the surface of the light bulb would have increased to about ten times the surface of the sun." [36]

So think about this for a moment. If a tiny 60-watt light bulb's light waves became coherent, the energy intensity would be ten times more than the energy intensity of the surface of the *sun*.

This is a striking example of the power of coherence. Our own energy becomes less scattered and more coherent when we stop draining it through Autopilot and Motor Mind. Coherence in the biological sense means the lining up of the body's energy and rhythms—the heart and brain waves, for example. "Entrainment" occurs when those rhythms become in synch.[37, 38]

The Institute of HeartMath researches biological coherence. Researchers there have found that the body's coherence increases through focusing on the breath and the heart area while putting attention on positive emotions.[39, 40]

This overlaps with what we know of the vagus nerve system and its overall calming effects. It underscores the power of reducing the static in our system by returning to the present and reconnecting to our breath.

This research also reminds us that where we put our attention really matters. If we use our internal choice muscles to focus on positive states while placing our attention on the breath and the heart, we can create positive shifts in our biology. We help the biological and energetic systems of our body come into greater coherence. We feel calmer and gain power, as well as enhance our health and wellbeing.

Coherence is more available to us when we connect to Being. Over-Doing in Autopilot can bring on Motor Mind and emotions that decrease our body's coherence. Our energy becomes scattered across the past and future as we disconnect from the body and the present. In this state, we are likely to feel more frustrated, irritable, self-doubting, and tense. These emotions and others common in stress and Autopilot do not support calm or coherence.

Conscious Calm tools help you reconnect to present time and to your body. You are no longer draining energy to the past, the future, and Autopilot Motor Mind activity.

Once you are more focused on Being and present time, you can choose to breathe more slowly and deeply, adding to your body's coherence. You more easily receive information from your Internal Guidance System, as you recognize what emotions are there and what information they hold. You then have choice to clear any static, adding again to your coherence and calm, and to your personal power.

This is similar to the spray of a garden hose. When our energy is leaking out all over the place with dramatic story lines about our emotions, with Motor Mind revved up and lousy boundaries between work and home life, it's like a leaky garden hose. The water is flowing through the hose, but it leaks at the same time. Its spray is weak and ineffective.

It's the same with our energy. Leaky energy scattered between past and future, up in the head and disconnected from the body, leaves us stressed, more scattered, and less effective.

But when we practice Being Breaks, and stop Motor Mind and Autopilot from running our life, we are plugging energy leaks. Then it's like water moving through a hose without losing any strength. The resulting spray will be a focused, steady, and powerful stream.

Once we plug the leaks and reconnect with our body and present time, we can use our energy better wherever we focus our attention. Our personal power is more fully engaged when our energy is more coherent.

Not only are we calmer, we also are more powerful and effective in our life.

So the tools we have discussed can do even more than guide you from stress to Conscious Calm. These tools also can add to your coherence, which can enhance your personal power, well being, and overall effectiveness.

Taking Steps on the Path

Discovering new ways of understanding stress and worry is helpful. Reading about the tools of Conscious Calm can be useful, too. You are learning methods for shifting inner patterns to bust old stress cycles for good.

But simply reading *about* these things has limited value. It's true that raising your awareness through new knowledge can begin to shift old patterns. You may notice your breathing more often, or realize more quickly when Motor Mind has taken off again. You may be able to feel static in your Internal Guidance System sooner, simply from reading the chapters on it and noticing this dynamic in your own experience.

However, if you are really ready to shake up old patterns of stress and worry, *taking action* is the key. If you are tired of draining your energy with Autopilot and Motor Mind, and truly want to reach new levels of personal power and calm, then taking concrete action is critical for your success.

One Small Step Is Not So Small

Changing old patterns of stress and worry can feel overwhelming. Some people decide that it's too much to try to change anything when they are so stressed out already. For some, it can feel like just another task on the long To-Do list.

I encourage you to look at this differently. There is a lot of information in this book. That was the idea—to give you information and tools so you can shift from feeling stressed out to calmer and more in control.

But where to start?

It's important to know that making even one small change can create cracks in a long-standing foundation of stress and worry. One small change often sets other changes in motion. Your decision to try just one Conscious Calm technique, to take just one action step, will dial up your awareness in other ways too. This can create a nice domino effect as other stress patterns fall. The next steps then feel easier as you experience relief and more inner strength.

So never underestimate the power of one, small-looking action. Strong energy can be behind the intention and choice to make that initial, modest step. Exercising that inner muscle of choice in your life can make all the difference.

Let's look at some specific ways a small, consistent shift in routine can break up some old habits, and make a difference in your level of calm, relaxation and control.

Mornings
Morning is one of the most potent times to bring your knowledge of Conscious Calm into action, and to decide to do something different.

This can start right when you wake up. See if you can notice where your thoughts are as you are waking up. What are you telling yourself first thing in the morning? How quickly does Motor Mind rev up? Are you aware of your body, or are you out of bed and in the shower or making coffee before you fully realize the day has started?

The first moments of the morning are an excellent time to choose Being instead of Autopilot Doing. For example, you could stay in bed for just a few minutes more and give yourself a first-thing–in-the-morning Being Break. Scan your body briefly and just notice what you feel. Don't add a story line to any of it; just see what you notice. Take ten slow, deeper breaths, and then be aware of how your body and mind respond.

Another way to foster Conscious Calm in the morning is to deliberately choose your pace. Maybe take ten slow, deep breaths first. Then when you decide to get up, do so more slowly than you usually would. Just take the pace down one or two notches.

This is a great way to keep your attention and awareness on the moment and on what you are actually doing. It allows you to be present with yourself, instead of heading into your morning routine with your mind already jumping to the future, draining your energy in the first few minutes you're awake!

Choosing just one of these can create a more conscious awakening, instead of allowing Autopilot to run your morning. It can set a different tone for your morning, and even for your entire day. With a small change, you claim your calm and well being as your priority, instead of vaulting into both internal and external Doing soon after you open your eyes.

Transitions

Transition times are another valuable place to add Being Breaks or other Conscious Calm tools.

Transitions in your day are easy to notice. For many people they are simple reminders to break up Autopilot Doing.

For instance, many people have a transition in the morning, from home to work. That one transition includes others—from home to a car, or from home to the train station or bus stop. Then there is yet another transition once you reach your destination.

These transitions can become opportunities for taking another step on the Conscious Calm path.

Instead of getting into the car, starting it up, and driving away, already thinking about what will happen later, you can interrupt that Autopilot inner Doing habit. You can choose Being instead. For example, before you leave home, you can pause and take several slow, deep breaths, and then walk out the door more aware of your surroundings.

Or, as you settle into your seat in the car (or bus or train), take a Being Break by breathing slowly and deeply ten times, and look around you. Can you notice the landscape as you go by? Many people report noticing for the first time details of the commute they have been doing for years, once they include Being Breaks in their commute routine. They realize they no longer arrive at work not remembering the ride itself.

If you are at home during the day, there are plenty of transitions there, too.

Some people use transitions to help themselves remember to integrate EFT into their day.

For example, just after getting up in the morning can be a good time for a round or two of tapping. You can tap on any tension you notice in your body, or any leftover static or emotion from a dream or a difficult night's sleep.

Just before a meal can be another easy time to do a round of EFT. Or between finishing one task and starting another. Many people find that doing EFT during transitions creates a good break during the day, and gives the body some needed relaxation.

Transitioning when you head home is another good time to take a Being Break, because it helps let go of any static from the day. It also helps create a good boundary between the work day and home life. Taking a Being Break or doing a round of EFT once you get home can help shake the stress-creating habit of continuing to think about work when your work day is over. It can help you enjoy your own space, and your family or friends, more fully. You will be more available to connect with them, too.

Evenings

Evenings are another time when taking a Being Break and practicing other Conscious Calm techniques can have a big impact.

One helpful method is to check your energy vectors—in which directions are your thought and feeling vectors pointed? Is anything still left over from the day? Is your thought and feeling energy tied up with something that happened five or six hours ago and is hard to let go of? Making the conscious choice to turn those vectors around is already a good start; you are deciding to return to present time. Your breath and EFT can both help with this.

Some people routinely do a few rounds of EFT before sleep, and find it helps remove leftover static from the day. Tapping at night can also help relax the body for deeper, more restful sleep.

More Doing-to-Being Activities

As we discussed in Chapter 10, some external activities can support Being and greater calm. These activities can help you shift out of too much mental Doing, when you notice Motor Mind has been going for a while. They also can be useful when you notice swirling emotion or static.

It's important, though, to notice where your attention is as you engage in any of these activities. If you go for a walk, be sure to notice where you put your attention. If your body is walking, but your mind is going over an argument from earlier in the day, this will not provide a Being Break. You will be dividing your attention, and you might return more worked up than when you left.

Engaging in one of these activities is not a Being Break if you do it on Autopilot. Bringing your entire self to the activity—your body and mind, your attention and awareness—allows these activities to support you on your path to Conscious Calm.

Here are a few examples; some of these are also in Chapter 10:

- Movement (dance, yoga, Chi Gong, Tai Chi)
- Exercise (walking, running, sports)
- Music (playing music or listening to it)
- Dancing (a class, a night out, or in your living room!)
- Art (creating art or viewing it)
- Crafts of all kinds
- Cooking or baking something special, or a recipe you have always wanted to try
- Time with pets
- Connecting with a friend you haven't spoken with for a while
- Playing with children
- Gardening or taking care of plants indoors
- Community activities that nourish you, whether a sport, a club, or a spiritual/religious gathering
- Time in nature, the master teacher of Being

These are a few possibilities. It can be helpful to create your own list of the activities you love that nourish you.

If it has been a while, and stressful times have led you to let go of some of these activities, see if you can add one of them back into your life in a more regular way. This will help you break up Autopilot Doing, return you to Being, and support you on the path of Conscious Calm.

Final Thoughts

While outside stress is real and can be daunting, you now know the secrets of stress and how inner stress works. You hold keys that can open the doors to Conscious Calm.

Although outside challenges will continue, and you may or may not have control over them, you always have the chance to choose greater inner control. Your personal power and your path to Conscious Calm lie in the inner choices you make from moment to moment.

You have the power to choose to engage both attention and awareness. You have the tools to pause Motor Mind, and to interrupt internal patterns that create more stress in your body and mind. And you have the knowledge and power to base your life more in Being instead of Autopilot Doing, enjoying more calm and centeredness.

Please keep in mind that this process can be like planting new seeds.

Seedlings take time, care, and the warmth of the sun to grow. The more you hold these attitudes with yourself on the Conscious Calm path, giving yourself a little time, taking steps with a caring attitude and some warmth (instead of judgment or impatience), the more the internal seeds you are planting will grow and thrive. Your steps on the path will become more sure and solid. The new internal choices will be easier and more natural as you grow in internal strength and centeredness.

As you walk the path of Conscious Calm, you will notice how much easier it is *not* to do so much of the internal busy work that you used to do. As you practice Being Breaks and breathing, you will become aware of the relief of not revving Motor Mind. You will feel the ease of not having so many dramatic stories in your mind. And you will notice the deep rest of connecting more to Being.

If you have been stressed out and worried for a while, you've been working very hard both externally and internally. My hope for you is that as you take your own steps toward Conscious Calm, you will find the relief and happiness you deserve, and embrace the calm, ease, and personal power that reflect who you really are.

Try This:

Dial up your awareness in the morning. What is your inner routine when you first wake up? What do you tell yourself? Where is your attention?

Remind yourself: "I have choice here too," and choose a Being Break or other Conscious Calm tool to practice in the morning. Stick with it for a week. Leave a note to yourself by your bed as a reminder. Notice how this changes your inner self-talk, the tone of your morning, and your feelings or mood as you start your day.

Resources

Try This!
Did you download your complimentary *Conscious Calm* "Try This!" Action Steps with with exercises plus additional questions and tips? If not, download them now by visiting:
http://consciouscalm.com/trythis

Connect with the Author
Visit www.lauramaciuika.com for the latest information about her writing, trainings and programs.

Follow the blog at www.consciouscalm.com

You can also follow Laura Maciuika on Twitter: @lauramaciuika or Like her Facebook page and stay in touch there:
www.facebook.com/lauramaciuika

Energy Psychology Resources, Including EFT
(Emotional Freedom Techniques)
http://myefttraining.com
Updated, affordable online EFT training by EFT originator Gary Craig.

www.energypsych.org
The Association of Comprehensive Energy Psychology (ACEP) website. Includes information on energy psychology research and practice, a listing of practitioners, and many other energy psychology resources in the U.S. and internationally.

www.eftuniverse.com
The primary world-wide site for EFT information, including practitioner listings.

www.innersource.net/ep/
Articles and additional energy psychology resources by David Feinstein, Ph.D.

www.tapintofreedom.com
Dr. Laura Maciuika's Integrative Psychotherapy site, with information about EFT and Energy Psychology, including selected research examples. Visit and sign up for the monthly Energy Works eNewsletter.

Additional resources for healing and personal growth

Robbins Madanes Center for Strategic Intervention
Founded by Anthony Robbins and Cloé Madanes. "Dedicated to promoting greater harmony and effectiveness in social systems ranging from families to corporations, and to government and nongovernmental organizations." www.robbinsmadanes.com

Innersource
Resources, training and information on energy psychology with David Feinstein, Ph.D. and energy medicine with Donna Eden. www.innersource.net

Tiller Foundation
Founded by William Tiller, PhD. to support experimental research and writing in psychoenergetics, including measuring the effects of human consciousness and intention. www.tillerfoundation.org

Trauma Center at Justice Resource Institute. Center founded and directed by Bessel van der Kolk, M.D. Resources, initiatives, research on trauma and healing. www.traumacenter.org

Somatic Experiencing
Trauma institute founded by Peter Levine, Ph.D. Includes resources and a practitioner listing. www.traumahealing.com

University of Massachusetts Medical Center, Center for Mindfulness in Medicine, Health Care, and Society. www.umassmed.edu/cfm

Pharmaceuticals, Mental Health, and Ethics

Kirch, Irving (2010). *The Emperor's New Drugs: Exploding the antidepressant myth*. New York: Basic Books.

Melody Peterson (2008). *Our Daily Meds*. New York: Sarah Crichton Books.

Whitaker, Robert (2010). *Anatomy of an Epidemic: Magic bullets, psychiatric drugs, and the astonishing rise of mental illness in America*. New York: Crown Publishing Group.

Open Medicine
www.openmedicine.ca
Mission: to facilitate the equitable, global dissemination of high-quality health research; to promote international dialogue and collaboration on health issues; to improve clinical practice; and to expand and deepen the understanding of health and health care.

Sample article:
Ethical considerations of publication planning in the pharmaceutical industry.
Adriane Fugh-Berman, MD, Susanna J. Dodgson, PhD.
http://www.openmedicine.ca/article/viewArticle/118/215

Additional Recommended Books

Benson, Herbert (2010). *The Relaxation Revolution: Enhancing your personal health through the science and genetics of mind-body healing*. New York: Scribner.

Craig, Gary (2008). *The EFT Manual*. Santa Rosa, CA: Energy Psychology Press.

Chodron, Pema (1997). *When Things Fall Apart: Heart Advice for Difficult Times*. Boston, MA: Shambala Publications.

----------------- (1994). *Start Where You Are: A Guide to Compassionate Living*. Boston, MA: Shambala Publications.

Church. Dawson. (2007). *Genie in your Genes: Epigenetic Medicine and the New Biology of Intention*. Santa Rose, CA: Elite Books.

Gallo, Fred (2007). *Energy Tapping for Trauma*. Oakland, CA: New Harbinger Publications

Gerath, Ruth (2010). *From Hired to Happy: The Secrets to a Vibrant Career and a Fulfilling Life*. Acton, MA: Hyde Street Publishing.

Hawkins, David R. (1998). *Power vs Force: An Anatomy of Consciousness*. Sedona, AZ: Veritas Publishing.

Kabat-Zinn, Jon (2005 edition). *Full Catastrophe Living : Using the wisdom of your body and mind to face stress, pain, and illness*. A program of the University of Massachusetts Medical Center/ Worcester. Stress Reduction Clinic. New York: Bantam Dell.

van der Kolk, Bessel. (Ed.). (2006 edition). *Traumatic Stress: The Effects of Overwhelming Experience on Mind, Body, and Society*. New York: Guilford Press.

Levine, Peter. (1997). *Waking the Tiger: Healing Trauma: The Innate Capacity to Transform Overwhelming Experiences*. Berkeley, CA: North Atlantic Books.

---------------- (2011). *In an Unspoken Voice: How the body releases trauma and restores goodness*. Berkeley, CA: North Atlantic Books.

Lipton, Bruce (2005). *Biology of Belief: Unleashing the Power of Consciousness, Matter, and Miracles.* Santa Rosa, CA: Mountain of Love/Elite Books.

Madanes, Cloé (2009). *Relationship Breakthrough: How to create outstanding relationships in every area of your life.* New York: Rodale, Inc.

Pert, Candace B. (1997). *Molecules of Emotion: Why you feel the way you feel.* New York: Scribner.

---------------------- (2006). *Everything You Need to Know to Feel Go(o)d.* Carlsbad, CA: Hay House.

Phillips, Maggie (2000). *Finding the Energy to Heal: How EMDR, Hypnosis, TFT, Imagery, and Body-Focused Therapy Can Help Restore Mindbody Health.* New York: Norton & Company.

Shimoff, Marci (2008). *Happy for No Reason: Seven steps to being happy from the inside out.* New York: Free Press.

Tiller, William (1997). *Science and Human Transformation.* Walnut Creek, CA: Pavior Publishing.

Williams, Angel Kyodo (2000). *Being Black: Zen and the art of living with fearlessness and grace.* New York: Penguin Group.

About the Author

Laura Maciuika is a clinical psychologist, teacher, and transformation mentor who has been bridging realities her entire life. Raised by Lithuanian parents, she spoke mainly Lithuanian at home and English outside. Visiting Lithuania as a child, a student, and later as a psychologist and teacher helped her learn how to move between world views, expanding her own as she supported other psychologists and teachers in broadening theirs. She began graduate school at the same time she began her training in mindfulness and meditation practices, and combined developmental and clinical psychology training with studies in energy healing modalities. A deep interest in inner transformation led to a dissertation on profound learning that changes people's relationship to themselves and to others, and ongoing study of inner transformation practices from across the world.

Dr. Maciuika's experience has included work in community mental health, a Latino Team of clinicians, HIV and free hospital clinics, schools, public health programs, as a clinical supervisor and administrator, as a Lecturer and Adjunct Professor, and as a workshop leader, and speaker on topics including developmental psychology, trauma and healing, stress management, and energy psychology. Dr.

Maciuika continues to combine world views and modalities in her work with people seeking freedom from stress and old patterns that no longer serve them. She also is the President of Tap Into Freedom Publishing, dedicated to books and programs on inner freedom. Dr. Maciuika continues to work in her Integrative Psychotherapy practice in northern California, and she also speaks and teaches about inner freedom and transforming your life to the next level of success and happiness.

Acknowledgements

Writing a book, although a solitary activity in ways, is supported, held, influenced and shaped by many others, both directly and indirectly. I would like to acknowledge and thank the following people for their help and support during this process of getting Conscious Calm developed, completed and out into the world:

My parents, who were ever their supportive and loving selves. Marcia Daft and Carrie Grossman, who provided helpful responses to early ideas for the work. Meg Turner gave invaluable feedback and insights on several drafts. Kathryn Geismar provided her skilled artist's eye and loving friend's direct feedback, especially about the directions and meanings of the cover art. Rasa Gustaitis and George Russell provided thoughtful responses on later drafts. Mary Foster created the EFT points drawing and shared discussions about writing in general. I would also like to thank Tom Antion, Sheela Bringi, Susan Daffron, George Foster, John Freedom, Ruth Gerath, John Maciuika, Cloé Madanes, Mariann Mohos, Bonnie Myhrum, Candace Pert, Maggie Phillips, Marci Shimoff, William Tiller, and angel Kyodo williams for their assistance, ideas, support and feedback.

Many others in the fields of psychology, energy psychology, energy medicine, and what is sometimes called "New Science" have shaped my understanding of the intricate organism of emotions, beliefs, matter, energy and consciousness that shape the human being. My respect and gratitude to Gary Craig, Roslyn Bruyere, David Feinstein, Fred Gallo, Bruce Lipton, Candace Pert, William Tiller, Dawson Church, Peter Levine, Donna Eden, Rupert Sheldrake, and Bessel van der Kolk for their work.

The Association of Comprehensive Energy Psychology continues to be a community of inspiration, and a beacon for research and practice regarding the dramatic healing techniques and modalities available within Energy Psychology. I honor ACEP members' commitment to realities and possibilities for healing the body-mind that shake and stretch the cultural canon of western psychological assumptions and techniques.

Conscious Calm would not have come to be without the many clients, students, and supervisees I have worked with over the years. Their courage in following their desire for a happier and freer life for themselves and for others has inspired me, and their paths and processes helped inform this book.

To my fellow volunteer participants with the network of charitable activities that is Embracing the World (www.embracingtheworld.org) in the U.S. and globally – you continue to inspire me to stretch ever further, and our service together is an ongoing, welcome challenge to walk my talk. I look forward to our continuing work together, and my gratitude to the many of you who have supported me on this part of the path.

Finally, to the founder of, and inspiration for, the international humanitarian work of Embracing the World – a Teacher who unwaveringly embodies the highest expressions of Conscious Calm – my deep and everlasting gratitude.

10% of all proceeds from the sales of *Conscious Calm* support the international humanitarian work of Embracing the World.

Embracing the World is a group of not-for-profit charities supporting communities with food, shelter, education, healthcare, and livelihood in over 30 countries.

www.embracingtheworld.org

Notes

Introduction – What This Book Is and Is Not About

[1]National Academies' Institute of Medicine report (2002). Unequal Treatment: Confronting Racial and Ethnic Disparities in Health Care. March 20, 2002.

[2]Karlsen, S. and Nazroo, J.Y. Relation Between Racial Discrimination, Social Class, and Health Among Ethnic Minority Groups. (2002). *American Journal of Public Health*. 92(4), 624-631.

[3]Ornish, D. (2008). The Toxic Power of Racism: Recent studies document the harmful effects of discrimination on our health. *Newsweek*, March 25, 2008. Retrieved 5/18/11 from http://www.newsweek.com/2008/03/24/the-toxic-power-of-racism.html

[4]Hatzenbuehler, M.L. (2011). The Social Environment and Suicide Attempts in Lesbian, Gay, and Bisexual Youth. *Journal of the American Academy of Pediatrics*. Published online April 11, 2011. Retrieved 5/18/11 from http://pediatrics.aappublications.org/content/early/2011/04/18/peds.2010-3020

Chapter 1 – Outside and Inside Stress

[5]American Institute of Stress (AIS). Retrieved 5/21/11, from:

http://www.stress.org/popular-keywords.htm

[6] Anderson, N.B. et al. (2010). Stress in America Findings. Washington, D.C.: American Psychological Association.

Chapter 2 – Autopilot and Motor Mind

[7] Wurman, S.A. (1987). *Information Anxiety*. New York: Doubleday, p. 32.

[8] American Psychological Association. Multitasking: Switching costs. Retrieved 5/14/11, from: http://www.apa.org/research/action/multitask.aspx

Chapter 4 – An Ally of Conscious Calm

[9] Chandler, B.A. The Gale Group Inc., from the *Gale Encyclopedia of Nursing and Allied Health* (2002). Retrieved 5/14/11, from: http://www.healthline.com/galecontent/stress-5

[10] Miller, L. (1994). *The Stress Solution*. New York: Simon and Schuster.

[11] American Psychological Association online Help Center. Life can take a toll on your body and mind. Retrieved 5/14/11, from: http://www.apa.org/helpcenter/mind-body.aspx

[12] Levine, P. (2011). *In an Unspoken Voice: How the body releases trauma and restores goodness*. Berkeley, CA: North Atlantic Books.

[13] HeartMD Institute (2010). Just Breathe: The simplest means of managing stress. Retrieved 3/11/11, from: http://www.heartmdinstitute.com/heart-healthy-lifestyles/mindbody-connection/just-breathe

Chapter 7 – Where Emotions Come In

[14] LeDoux, J.E. (2000). Emotion circuits in the brain. *Annual Review of Neuroscience*. 23, 155-184.

[15] Ochsner, K. N. and Feldman Barret, L. (2000). A Multiprocess Perspective on the Neuroscience of Emotion. In T.

Mayne & G. Bonnano (Eds.), *Emotion: Current Issues and Future Directions*. New York: Guilford Press.

[16]Angell, M. (2005). *The Truth About the Drug Companies*. New York: Random House Trade Paperback Edition.

[17] BMJ-British Medical Journal (2008, June 20). Should Doctors Be 'Selling' Drugs For The Pharmaceutical Industry? *Science Daily*.

[18] Ioannidis JPA (2005). Why Most Published Research Findings Are False. PLoS Med 2(8): e124. doi:10.1371/journal.pmed.0020124

[19] Benson, L. (2010). Groups want tighter controls over drug industry influence. Retrieved 11/8/10, from: http://minnesota.publicradio.org/display/web/2010/01/25/pharmaceutical-legislation/

[20]Pert, C. D. (1997). *Molecules of Emotion: Why you feel the way you feel*. New York: Scribner.

[21] Ibid, 148.

[22]Ibid, 188.

Chapter 8 – Working with Emotions

[23]Davis, M., Eshelman, E.R., McKay, M. (2008). *The Relaxation & Stress Reduction Workbook*. Oakland, CA: New Harbinger Publications.

[24]Goldstein, J. *The Experience of Insight* (1987). Boston: Shambala.

[25] Rosenburg, L. (1999). *Breath by Breath: The liberating practice of Insight Meditation*. Boston: Shambala.

Chapter 9 – Static in Our Internal Guidance System

[26] Pert, C., Ibid.

[27] Kandel, ER (2007). *In Search of Memory - The Emergence of a New Science of Mind.* New York: WW Norton & Company.

Chapter 10 – Clearing the Static, Part I
[28] Csikszentmihalyi, M. (1997).*Finding Flow: The Psychology of Engagement with Everyday Life.* New York: Basic Books, 1997.

Chapter 11 – Clearing the Static, Part II

[29]Feinstein, D. (2008). Energy Psychology: A Review of the Preliminary Evidence. *Psychotherapy: Theory, Research, Practice, Training.* 45(2), 199-213.

[30]Freedom, J. (August, 2011). Energy Psychology: The Future of Therapy? Institute of Noetic Sciences: *Noetic Now,* Issue 13.

[31]Craig, G. (2008). *The EFT Manual.* Santa Rosa, CA: Energy Psychology Press.

[32]Church, D. and Brooks, A. Application of Emotional Freedom Techniques. *Integrative Medicine: A Clinician's Journal,* (2010), Aug/Sep, 46-48.

[33]Burke, L. Single Session EFT for Stress-Related Symptoms After Motor Vehicle Accidents. *Energy Psychology: Theory, Research, & Treatment,* (2010), 2(1), 65-72.

[34]Rowe, J. (2005). The Effects of EFT on Long-term Psychological Symptoms. *Counseling and Clinical Psychology Journal,* 2(3):104.

Chapter 12 – Walking the Path

[35]Tiller, W.A. (1997).*Science and Human Transformation.* Walnut Creek, CA: Pavior Publishing.

[36]W. Tiller, personal communication, May 18, 2011.

[37]Tiller, 1997, p. 223.

[38] Institute of HeartMath. Coherence, Emotions and Interconnectedness: Coherence. Retrieved 3/28/11, from: http://www.heartmath.org/research/research-home/coherence. html?submenuheader=0

[39]McCraty,R., Atkinson, M., Tiller, W.A., Rein, G., and Watkins, A.D. The Effects of Emotions on Short-Term Power Spectral Analysis of Heart Rate Variability. (1995). *American Journal of Cardiology.* 1995; 76 (14): 1089-1093.

[40]McCraty, R., Tiller, W.A., Atkinson, M. Head-Heart Entrainment: A Preliminary Survey. (Feb., 1996). Paper presented at the Key West Brain-Mind, Applied Neurophysiology, EEG Biofeedback 4th Annual Advanced Colloquium, Key West, FL.

Index

Share Conscious Calm with a Friend or Colleague

Please send me:

                         Price Sub-total

                         Conscious Calm: Keys to $17.95 $_____

Quantity: _____   *Freedom from Stress and Worry*

                         Shipping: $5.00 for first book, $2.00
for each additional book for U.S. orders.
For international orders, $9.00 for first
book, $2.00 each additional (estimate) $_____

                         Sales tax: Please add 8.75% for books $_____
shipped to a California address

                                        Total: $_____

Please also send me more FREE information on:

[ ] Other products/programs [ ] Consulting [ ] Speaking/Seminars

_____

Email address for additional info/Order confirmation

_____ Check enclosed with order

_____ Please charge my credit card:

                  [ ] Visa   [ ] MasterCard [ ] American Express

Name on card: _____

Card Number: _____

Expiration Date: _____

Buyer's Address: _____

Shipping Address: _____
                         (if different)

Fax Orders: 888-961-3997 Fax this form.

Email orders: orders@tapintofreedompublishing.com

Mail orders: Tap Into Freedom Publishing, LLC, 4096 Piedmont Ave., Suite 365, Oakland, CA 954611-0550, USA Telephone: 888-741-1811

CPSIA information can be obtained at www.ICGtesting.com
Printed in the USA
BVOW07s0209091013

333284BV00007B/39/P